A YORKSHIRE DIARY

A YORKSHIRE DIARY
Year of Crisis

DAVID BAIRSTOW
with Derek Hodgson

Photographs by Barry Wilkinson

SIDGWICK & JACKSON
LONDON

First published in Great Britain in 1984
by Sidgwick & Jackson Limited

Copyright © 1984 David Bairstow
All photographs © Barry Wilkinson, Picture House Limited, Bradford

ISBN 0-283-99109-7

Typeset by Tellgate Ltd., London N6
Printed in Great Britain by
Biddles Ltd., Guildford, Surrey
for Sidgwick & Jackson Limited,
1 Tavistock Chambers, Bloomsbury Way
London WC1A 2SG

To my dad, Des

The Principal Characters

Bairstow, Gail: *Wife to David and fiercely supportive. Family nickname: Stormy.*

Boycott, Geoffrey: *One of Yorkshire's greatest players and a record-breaker in Tests. Idolized by his many supporters, blamed for Yorkshire's decline by many critics. Is he Batman? Is he Borgia? Read on.*

Callaghan, John: *Cricket correspondent of the* Yorkshire Evening Post *and author of several books on Yorkshire cricket. Sharp critic of the former Committee.*

Carrick, Philip: *Yorkshire's slow left-arm bowler and a useful batsman in this period. Like Bairstow, a Bradfordian. An old friend of the author, whom Bairstow was reluctant to drop from the team. Nickname: Fergie.*

Close Brian: *Former Yorkshire and England captain who became the new Chairman of the Cricket Sub-Committee (in effect an unpaid team manager) after the Revolution. Totally fearless, completely outspoken and therefore no politician.*

Crawford, Michael: *Chairman of the former Committee and former Treasurer of the Club. A moderating influence, greatly missed after his resignation.*

Fielden, Sidney: *Leader of the pro-Boycott forces in the Revolution who then became Chairman of the Public Relations Sub-Committee. Detective sergeant and lay preacher. Cromwellian orator who won great respect after the Revolution by* *sticking rigidly to all his campaign promises. Most memorable quote: 'Geoffrey is not always right.'*

Hampshire, John: *Brilliant Yorkshire batsman and former county captain who emigrated to Derbyshire after two years in the cross-fire. Strongly anti-Boycott. Nickname: Hamps.*

Hartley, Neil: *Modest, yet very talented all-rounder who was chosen by Ray Illingworth as a future Yorkshire captain. This put him in a similar position to the Archduke Franz Ferdinand in Sarajevo in 1914. Nickname: Tommy.*

Hopps, David: *Cricket correspondent of the* Yorkshire Post *and therefore the most influential media voice in the county. Did not succeed Terry Brindle, a supporter of Boycott, until after the Revolution. His personal opinions were being formed in this period.*

Hutton, Richard: *Son of Sir Leonard and a Yorkshire and England cricketer in his own right. Hostile to Boycott's captaincy from the appointment and an opponent ever since. Nickname: Archie.*

Illingworth, Raymond: *A Yorkshire and England player who left the county after a contract dispute to lead Leicestershire and England in a triumphant career. Returned to Yorkshire as manager and then, succeeding Old, as captain. According to the pro-Boycott forces his principal task, as set by the old Committee, was to get rid of Boycott. A BBC TV commentator in this period. Nickname: Illy.*

Kirk, Reg: *Represented Hull on the old Committee. A vociferous critic, he succeeded Michael Crawford as Chairman after the Revolution. With Fielding a firm believer in 'returning the Club to the members'.*

Lister, Joe: *Yorkshire's secretary and chief executive, who had many clashes with the pro-Boycott forces during the Revolution.*

Tried to steer a middle course between the Illingworth and Boycott factions, stayed in office and has continued to survive.

Moxon, Martyn: *Opening batsman whose career, some say, was delayed by the Civil War. Talented player who was chosen by England during this period. Shy, able, with a good brain and an outstanding prospect as a future captain. Nickname: Froggy.*

Nicholson, Tony: *Highly capable Yorkshire seam bowler of the previous era. Strongly formative influence on the young Bairstow and his generation. A player much saddened by the strife. Nickname: Nick.*

Old, Chris: *Very high-class all-rounder who, in Mike Brearley's words was 'a displaced gene away from greatness'. Briefly succeeded Hampshire as captain before giving way to Illingworth and then joining Warwickshire. Equally critical of Boycott and Illingworth. Nickname: Chilly.*

Oldham, Steve: *Experienced seam bowler who was brought back from Derbyshire by Illingworth, before his departure. A bowling coach whom Bairstow had to use almost non-stop as a bowler. Elder statesman of the dressing room. Nickname: Esso.*

Padgett, Doug: *Former Yorkshire and England batsman who became Yorkshire's coach. A Bradfordian and friend and contemporary of Illingworth.*

Sellers, Brian: *Former Yorkshire captain and Chairman of the Cricket Sub-Committee at the start of the author's career. Strong disciplinarian, last of the Yorkshire warlords and the man who sacked Illingworth and Close.*

Sharpe, Phillip: *Former Yorkshire and England batsman and an England selector in this period. One of the few former Committee members to retain his seat in the Revolution. Member of the Cricket Sub-Committee that sacked Boycott.*

Sidebottom, Arnie: *The team's senior all-rounder and an England player of mercurial form, ranging within hours from Test to club class. Much of Yorkshire's fortunes in this period depended on his form and fitness. Nickname: Stevo or Moonbeam.*

Trueman, Fred: *Great Yorkshire and England fast bowler who lost his Committee seat in the Revolution after some outspoken public attacks on Boycott. Member of the Cricket Sub-Committee that sacked Boycott.*

Warner, David: *Cricket correspondent of the* Bradford Telegraph and Argus *and a winner of a newspaper award for his reporting of the Revolution. Inclined towards the old Committee, which had strong Bradford and Bradford-based sympathies.*

Prologue

As far away as New Zealand and California the news made headlines. Geoff Boycott, former Yorkshire captain, had won with his supporters a resounding victory over a county club committee studded with famous names. At a special general meeting, called at Harrogate's luxurious conference centre in January 1984, a band of men that included a detective sergeant lay preacher, a Queen's Counsel, a theatre administrator, accountants, printers and a shop steward sent into exile a governing body that included some of the most celebrated figures in English cricket, such as Norman Yardley and Freddie Trueman.

It was seven days that shook the cricket world, a storming of the Yorkshire's own Winter Palace that left me, David Bairstow, exposed on all sides. Appointed captain to succeed Ray Illingworth, a major target for the rebels who were now the committee, I knew that I had to serve as the link between the old and the new, between the pro- and anti-Boycott factions who, on the evidence of the voting figures, divided the county almost equally.

Being captain of Yorkshire has more than once been described as 'the second best job on earth'; the first being the captaincy of England. I doubt if many Yorkshire captains, certainly in recent years, would agree with that. The pressures from the public and from members for a successful team are so strong and have been unsatisfied for so long that every match is played in an atmosphere of

1

crisis. That alone makes the leadership of Yorkshire a daunting task. In addition, the captain has to work with Geoffrey Boycott. An American lady, trying to explain to her television audience what the row was all about, summed it up as, 'All the guy wants to do is play ball.' I wish it were that simple.

So this is the story of a year and what came before: how I arrived at this point in my life; and how my career expanded among the players and the watchers, public and press who make up what must be the most fractious, exasperating, jealous, arrogant, and certainly the greatest cricket club in the world.

Harrogate:
The Storming of the Winter Palace

The trouble with revolutions is that anyone can be caught up in them. A member of the former Yorkshire Club Committee, peering out from the balcony across the field at Headingley, pointed to me and said to his companion, 'That's the little bastard who's causing all the trouble. Bairstow's the head of the Yorkshire mafia.'

That remark was made to another member of the committee and, such was the unity and sense of purpose among them, that I had heard about it within hours. The accusation stung, especially because I thought that I was doing my best to steer clear of all politics and to play for Yorkshire.

But whether we liked it or not, the players were dragged into the war. We had been asked, in a dressing-room poll, whether we wanted Geoffrey Boycott in the team. I, along with Graham Stevenson and Arnie Sidebottom, had voted 'Yes'. The others all voted 'No'. So, we three were immediately branded as 'Boycott men', which was a distortion of our position. But in a war there can be no greys, only blacks and whites.

To understand Yorkshire's civil war it is important first

to accept that the fighting wasn't all about whether Boycott stayed with the club. The Yorkshire Club has always been split by factions, dating right back to its foundation in 1863. It may indeed be that the only time the club has been fully united has been during the successful years, and there were plenty of those. Even at the beginning there was a furious row between Sheffield, where the club began, and Leeds, as the county's leading city, and there might not have been a county club of any kind but for the arrival of two dictators who were prepared to knock quarrelling heads together.

The first was Lord Hawke, who established discipline in a wonderfully talented but erratic side – 'a team of alecans' they were called – and then ruled the club with an iron grip. Hawke's momentum gave the club a tide of success that carried them into the 1930s when another warlord, Brian Sellers, re-launched the side into an even more consistently successful phase.

It's hard to understand the scale of that success today. Between 1919 and 1939 Yorkshire won the championship, then the only trophy available, twelve times in twenty years. An England team always included three or four Yorkshiremen, sometimes as many as five. A Yorkshire defeat created as much stir in those days as an upset for Liverpool Soccer Club does today. A player who made a century against Yorkshire, or who took five or more wickets, was an automatic candidate for a Test place.

It was Geoffrey Boycott's bad luck in 1971 to become captain of a team that would win nothing. But this was not merely because the team was not strong. The 1960s were the last years of the old county championship, again dominated by a Yorkshire led by Brian Close, and county cricket was about to be turned upside down.

Sponsors appeared, particularly for one, two, and finally three, one-day competitions. Sponsors appeared for individual county clubs. No sponsor can afford to be associated with failure, so some strong and unusual pressures were exerted on Lord's.

County sides were placed on a more or less level footing

4

by permitting the introduction of overseas players; Yorkshire insisted on their players being born inside the pre-1974 boundaries. All pitches were covered, making it far less likely that a batting side would be caught on a rain-affected surface; Yorkshire's great strength had always rested in spin bowlers, who all but disappeared. Finally MCC, who had always controlled the game world-wide in the interests purely of cricket, were forced to give way to a new government, the Test and County Cricket Board, whose primary purpose was to raise enough money to keep county clubs solvent and to pay Test players sufficient to prevent them deserting to pirate ventures.

All this meant that Yorkshire slipped further and further from the centre of the county game. Close had been sacked as captain in 1970 because he openly dissented with the direction the game was taking. Although a majority of the then committee was almost certainly in tacit agreement with him, Sellers decided that he needed a captain more attuned to modern ambitions. This was the second of two monumental errors.

The first had been to allow Ray Illingworth to leave for Leicestershire in 1968. He wanted a contract of more than one year, which is all that was ever offered to Yorkshire players in those days. The departure of Illingworth and Close following closely that of such players as Jimmy Binks, Ken Taylor, Bryan Stott and Freddie Trueman meant that the heart of the team had gone within five years.

Within a few years the remnants of the 1960s team, Phil Sharpe, Don Wilson, Richard Hutton and Tony Nicholson, were to follow by retiring. Neither Lord Hawke nor Brian Sellers could have won very much with the team that was available in the mid-1970s, and against the opposition that they had to face.

I shall recount the difficulties of those years – and a few laughs – in later pages. All this is the preamble to the actual outbreak of hostilities, which began in earnest when Boycott was sacked from the captaincy in 1978, following Illingworth's return to manage the team. There is no doubt

5

in my mind that Illy, a highly successful England and Leicestershire captain, was brought back to remove Boycott. He would have succeeded, I believe, in any county but Yorkshire.

A Reform Group of dissident members had been formed back in 1970 after the Close sacking, though they could never muster much support from the majority of members. But as lean year followed lean year both members and the public became more and more discontented and the Reform Group gathered enough strength to force a special general meeting. In the wake of Boycott's removal from the captaincy, they won the day in the hall at Harrogate, but were beaten on the proxy vote of those members who did not attend.

Because of the factionalism in the county, which I mentioned earlier, Yorkshire is governed by a General Committee that is elected on a district basis – three members for Leeds, one for York, and so on. I don't think that even the former committee could deny that they were self-perpetuating, and that vacancies tended to be filled by friends or associates of committee members.

The constitution of the club protected the General Committee from a total overthrow by decreeing that only one-third of the twenty-four directly elected members should stand each year. So the establishment, if you like, was always confident of an in-built majority even when the odd dissenters appeared.

All this was thrown into total confusion in 1983 when the committee, with two apparently contradictory decisions, gave Boycott a testimonial in 1984 and then announced they would not be renewing his contract. They thus succeeded in enraging just about everyone.

The decision to sack Boycott came from the Cricket Sub-Committee, entirely composed of old players such as former captains Ronnie Burnet and Billy Sutcliffe, and former players such as Don Brennan and Freddie Trueman. They were all to lose their seats in the March election.

The decision to give Boycott a testimonial, marking his

twentieth year as a Yorkshire player, came from the General Committee which included three members, Reg Kirk (Hull), Peter Charles (Rotherham), and Sid Fielden (Doncaster), who were the leading lights of the rebel Reform Group, soon to be renamed Yorkshire Members 1984.

A furious war developed in public meetings and in the media. Writs flew like confetti. Moderate voices, like those of president Norman Yardley and chairman Michael Crawford, whose concern was for the unity of the club, were drowned out in the hubbub.

The Cricket Sub-Committee insisted that Boycott's sacking was a cricketing decision taken on the advice of manager Ray Illingworth, supported by them unanimously. Famous former players such as Sir Leonard Hutton agreed with them. The rebels on the other hand said that it was inhuman to sack the county's most prominent player and that Illingworth, not Boycott, should go.

Three motions went before another special general meeting at Harrogate in January: that Boycott should be reinstated; that the meeting had no confidence in the General Committee; and that there was no confidence in the Cricket Sub-Committee. The rebels won all three votes, not substantially, but by enough to make the General Committee decide that all, not one-third, should stand for re-election.

By the time of the annual general meeting, at Sheffield in March, the revolution was complete. Almost all the old committee had been wiped out, though the margin in some cases was tiny – Burnet lost Harrogate by four votes. Illingworth was sacked, club treasurer David Welch resigned only a few days after being re-elected in Sheffield, and the exchange of committee members with the Leeds Club (the landlords at Headingley) was ended.

As the new captain, in succession to Illingworth, Old, Boycott, and Hampshire, I could not complain. Among the new committee members was Brian Close, my first county captain, now restored as chairman of the Cricket Sub-

7

Committee in place of Burnet. Close insisted that I should have the right to pick the team, at the same time implying that if I got it wrong I should have to answer to him, an arrangement I regarded as fair.

There remained Boycott, now a member of the new committee and clearly, as many of his fellow members had ridden to power on his coat-tails, a powerful one. How would he fit into the team? How would he regard my authority? Or, come to that, Close's?

What is often overlooked with Geoff Boycott is that when he says Yorkshire cricket is his life he is telling the truth. I don't know what he plans to do when he does finish playing, and he is fit enough to go on playing for years yet, but I do know he will find retirement a heartbreak. When the decision to sack him was made, he rang me as, I suppose, one of his oldest friends and supporters in the dressing room. He was obviously very shaken by the decision, which he hadn't expected. After a while he broke off the conversation. He was so choked up I thought he might have been crying.

There was something like fifteen years between my first conversation with Boycott and that one. The writer of a soap opera could easily have drawn a thread between one and the other. But life is never quite like that. . .

. . . And I love life. It has been seldom sweeter than back in June 1970 when, as a mere seventeen-year-old, I heard the news that I had been chosen to play for Yorkshire. My chief concern at that time was to pass my 'A' levels at Hanson Grammar, Bradford, so I was studying at the local public library when Barry Wilkinson, who has taken the pictures for this book, called to tell me of my selection. After an initial misunderstanding as to whether I had been chosen for the first, or as I had assumed, the second team, Barry and I set off to celebrate. Two pints later I went to see my maths master, Laurie Bennett, the man who had persuaded me to stay on at school after my 'O' levels. He dispatched me to see the Head to ask if I could bring my 'A' levels forward, offering a packet

8

of mints and adding, 'You'd better try to kill that beer on your breath.'

I sat those exams at six o'clock in the morning before my first championship match, against Gloucestershire at Bradford. The Deputy Head then drove me up to the cricket ground, Park Avenue. It was a different world. Geoff Boycott, driving up in a yellow Volvo, called to me by the gate, where I was very proudly leaving some match tickets for my father, 'Morning, David. Will you carry this for me?'

I took the bag and marched with him up to the dressing room where he motioned for me to put down his gear.

'Thank you, you can go now.'

'Go?' I queried. 'I'm playing.'

Geoff was taken aback, 'I didn't know.'

As a Colt I had practised with Boycott and had been pleased to do so. I had heard all about his famous temperament, but I had got on fairly well with him and wanted to continue that way. It wasn't long before I realized that my appreciation of him wasn't universally shared. A book written on Yorkshire cricket was to describe my walking on the field, 'with a paternal arm around Geoffrey Boycott's shoulder'. On reading that, one of Yorkshire's senior writers is said to have observed, 'It should have been around his bloody neck.'

I was soon to observe the impact Boycott had on the Yorkshire dressing room. In a John Player League game at Hull, Boycott was lbw to a ball from 'Butch' White of Hampshire that shot straight across the ground: everyone rushed out of the Yorkshire dressing room, leaving me on my own. As they fled through the door, I asked why, and was told, 'This will not be a pleasant place to be for a while.' It wasn't!

When the Yorkshire players stayed in the dressing room, I found them a friendly crowd, especially Richard Hutton and Don Wilson. I soon learned to laugh at John Hampshire's dry humour. 'Hamps' had a genius for nicknames: Chris Old (C.Old) became 'Chilly'. Steve Oldham (S. Oldham) became 'Esso'. He took one look at my red hair and, calling on his Australian experiences, dubbed me 'Bluey'. Later it was John, along with two or three other Yorkshire players, who added a second nickname, 'Stanley', after the author Stanley Barstow. By this time I was known as 'Bluey' to the public, and in the closed society of a dressing room that inevitably led to the coining of a new and 'in' nickname.

As a Bradfordian I drifted toward my 'towny' in the side, Douglas Padgett, who drove me around in the days before I could use a car myself. I and another Bradford lad in the team, Phil Carrick, always called Tony Nicholson 'Dad'. I think he revelled in the paternal role, quietly, and wasn't above handing out a quick clip round the ear if he thought we'd done anything wrong. 'I can still feel my head ringing,' Philip remembers.

Brian Close was captain in my first season, but he was in and out of the side because of a shoulder injury he had sustained diving in to the crease when running a quick single with Richard Hutton. He came back against Sussex at Leeds, was again batting with Richard, again went for a risky single, again had to dive in and again put his shoulder out. He was not very pleased.

I got my first rollicking from him during the Surrey game at Bradford. Intikhab came on to bowl and, never having seen a leg-spinner before, I fancied my chances. Down the wicket I went and lifted him twice into the car park. Back went the fielders but I thought I could do it again and was caught, inevitably, at long on. Having scored 26 I was quite pleased with myself, until the captain came storming through from the front dressing room, picked me up, pinned me against the wall, waved his finger in front of my nose and filled my ears with asterisks. The gist of it all was that I had been a very stupid little boy.

Of course, I'd heard a lot about Brian Close. Six foot two inches, fifteen stone, an awesome, fearless man, and a very strong character. I'd heard all the legends about his smoking and drinking. We were leaving Scarborough to drive down to Brighton, and I was supposed to be travelling with Boycott and Hampshire. Then Boycott said to me, 'You're travelling with Closey.'

I replied, 'Well, you rotten sod. You've stuffed me. I've heard about his driving. He'll frighten me to death.'

We climbed into a brown Capri and set off down the Driffield Road, with Close pedalling along at his usual rate, a speed I won't dare mention, when we came to a sharp left-hand turn followed by a fairly steep incline. The Capri carried so much gear it wasn't

10

balanced, and the next thing I knew we were broadsiding down this hill with a big wagon coming up towards us. I honestly thought my end had come. I was praying when somehow Close managed to steer the car off the road and up a grass verge inches away from a wall that surrounded a cemetery. All I could see was gravestones!

A fellow approached the car; I wound down the window.

'Are you all right?' he asked.

'Yes, thanks,' I said, although I felt anything but.

'You should have more bloody sense than to drive like that,' he muttered as he marched away.

Close, totally unconcerned, then turned to me, 'I'm glad he came to your side. He might have recognized me.'

By May 1971 I felt established in the Yorkshire side. In the Whitsuntide Roses match against Lancashire I took six catches in the first innings, equalling the then county record held by David Hunter, Jimmy Binks and Reg Allen. I took another three catches in the second innings, but it then rained so hard that Farokh Engineer, the Lancashire and India wicket-keeper, proclaimed, in his deep Bombay accent and to our great amusement, 'God is a Yorkshireman.'

Geoff Boycott had succeeded Brian Close as captain, Close having made it plain what he thought about the new and increasing emphasis on one-day cricket and losing his job as a result. Boycott was on a pinnacle: he had just returned from Australia where injury had prevented him from overtaking the great Don Bradman's record (he missed it by only 19) of the highest aggregate during an Australia-England series. Geoff took over Yorkshire as if determined to stamp his authority on the side from the start and, looking back, I think he would agree with me that he might have approached things a little differently.

Two things happened. Boycott personally went from strength to strength. He hit 2,200 runs that season averaging 105.76, the first batsman ever to top the 100 in a domestic season. And the Yorkshire team, the remnants of the side that had won seven championships and two Gillette Cups between 1959 and 1969, was finally broken up.

It wasn't entirely due to a lack of empathy between the captain and senior players. In the late sixties and early seventies many experienced cricketers were overtaken by the extra physical demands of one-day cricket and, lacking much sympathy for a form of the game they tended to disparage – 'electric rounders' was one popular term – they drifted out of a game they were finding hard to recognize. Above all, supreme fitness was needed; a thirty-two-year-old in the game today is much fitter than his counterpart ten or twelve years ago.

Douglas Padgett, Phil Sharpe, Don Wilson and Richard Hutton all went, and for varying reasons, although in Richard's case there was no trying to disguise the feelings he had for the captain. Hutton and Boycott were totally conflicting personalities and the situation was never eased by Richard's acidulous sense of humour. I can laugh with anyone, but I admit there were times when I found him hard to take: for instance, when he was taking the mickey out of my accent. Soon only Tony Nicholson and John Hampshire were left, along with Geoff Boycott, of Close's near-invincibles.

Close's departure had been almost the last act of Brian Sellers. Sellers, the legendary Yorkshire captain of pre-war days who won championships as a matter of course and regularly led seven or eight Test players, was a fierce disciplinarian. When I first met him he was chairman of the Cricket Sub-Committee and easily the most powerful and influential man in the club.

He saw me one Monday morning and told me to get my hair cut. He saw me again on Tuesday morning and asked me why I was waiting. I made some excuse about not having a car and he said, 'Get it cut. I've made an appointment for you.' Then he named a hairdressers in Bradford and told me that I had to catch a bus and report there the following morning.

'Come in, David,' said the barber. 'I've been expecting you. This one's on the house.' It was, too. I came out looking like a ginger billiard ball. I doubt if I had a single hair longer than a quarter-inch. Back at Headingley Mr Sellers growled at me: 'Right. Tha' looks like a lad now.'

That was the kind of discipline that existed in county cricket at that time and there are many players who will tell you that all idea of discipline had gone long before I even entered the game.

Mike Bore, from Hull, became Don Wilson's intermittent replacement in the Yorkshire side, bowling slow to medium left arm, Underwood-style. Mike, a very genial character sometimes known as 'Noddy', was the greatest authority on fish and chips in the East Riding and had a positive genius for getting on the wrong side of the new captain.

At Middlesbrough in 1972 Yorkshire had to lend Gloucestershire a fielder and Noddy took his place at long leg. Boycott was 68, hooked a bouncer from Procter and was caught – at long leg. Instead of staying on the boundary and looking sheepish, in marched Bore with a big grin to join the celebrating Gloucestershire fielders. When he got back to the Yorkshire dressing room he found his irate captain had picked up Bore's cricket bag and thrown it into the opposition room.

That was also the year that Essex laid a plan to deal with Boycott, who had hit them for 260 not out and 232 in the two preceding years. Keith Boyce was instructed to give Boycott a bouncer, first ball, which he did. Boycott rose like a trout, hooked, the ball flew off his gloves straight to the Essex captain and wicket-keeper, 'Tonker' Taylor. Taylor promptly dropped it, picked it up and flipped it back to Boyce as if nothing had ever happened. If ever a plan went awry, that was one: for Boycott went on to hit them for 121 and 86 in the match.

Boyce, a West Indian fast bowler and hurricane hitter, is also remembered for his war with Richard Hutton. Richard, in his inimitable fashion, had said something derogatory in Boyce's hearing. Whether it was about West Indians, or fast bowlers, or even Chelmsford fish and chips, we never knew, but for a couple of years Boyce carried a photograph of Hutton in his top pocket.

A good summer was spoiled by the disappointment of losing the 1972 Benson & Hedges Final to Ray Illingworth's Leicestershire. We were confident: we had played well in the earlier rounds, but by the time we reached Lord's we were without Boycott and Wilson, both injured, while Barrie Leadbeater batted for a long time with a damaged hand.

13

In 1973 I was capped – always a very proud moment for any Yorkshire player. It was a red-hot day at Chesterfield, but I still went out wearing my new sweater with its bands of Cambridge and Oxford blue and gold.

Yorkshire played an astonishing tied match with Middlesex at Bradford, and Graham Stevenson made his debut for Yorkshire. Don Wilson, seeing his big smiling face appear round the corner of the dressing-room door, had nicknamed him 'Moonbeam'.

John Hampshire, as chief hoaxer, told young Graham that the first day of every Park Avenue match meant black pudding and peas for lunch, and that it was twelfth man's task to collect them for the dressing room.

Off went Graham to the caterers who, naturally, were mystified, but suggested that there might be a stall on the ground that sold black pudding and peas. We were able to follow Graham's progress round the ground from the dressing-room window and managed to keep straight faces when a thoroughly exasperated and red-faced young Moonbeam returned to declare he couldn't find any bloody black pudding anywhere on Park Avenue.

This was also the summer of Yorkshire's defeat by Durham in the Gillette Cup at Harrogate. We were all out for 135. Durham celebrated for ages and deserved every moment. We were castigated and deserved every word.

Curiously, we did have our best John Player League season to date, finishing second, winning eleven of our sixteen matches. Boycott and Hampshire, who opened regularly on Sundays, shared 1,200 runs. Chris Old was a formidable number three or four, and John Woodford did a good steady job with bat and ball.

That year was a very special one for me as I married Gail on 30 August. We spent the winter very happily in South Africa, where I coached for Transvaal, played for the University of Witwatersrand and managed to do some work in Soweto.

The following summer, in Bath, I was introduced to a smiling, stocky West Indian who, I was told, might one day become a Test batsman. 'Good luck,' I said. I hoped he doesn't remember that as being patronizing. His name was Viv Richards.

14

Richard Hutton upset Basil D'Oliveira at Hull – there was controversy over an lbw decision denied our off-spinner, Geoff Cope – and Dolly hammered us all over the East Riding, for 227.

Barrie Leadbeater, a Yorkshire batsman of those days who could soon become a leading Test umpire, entered the story at Scarborough. He was fielding slip and, such was his admiration for Colin Cowdrey who made a fine 122, Barrie broke into spontaneous applause at every good shot, and there were plenty. The other Yorkshire players found it not a little disconcerting.

Barrie had then been playing with Yorkshire for eight years, had been capped in 1969, after a particularly outstanding Gillette Cup Final innings, but still hadn't scored a first-class century. On this occasion he had reached 98 when he faced the last ball of the hundredth over, then the mandatory closure on first innings. Kent, I'm sure, would have been quite happy to see him get his long-delayed century as he played that ball down to fine leg. But instead of dashing off to scramble a second, Barrie ambled a single, and to this day maintains he was happier being 99 not out rather than risking a run out at that score.

Oh yes, the Leadbeater 100 did arrive the following year, but even that was not straightforward. Hampshire, the county, batted all one Saturday at Portsmouth. On Sunday, Yorkshire won a John Player League fixture at Bournemouth. Returning to Portsmouth on the Monday, they found someone had dug up the pitch. Special dispensation was granted by Lord's for a new wicket to be cut and Barrie, not out on Saturday night, went on to make 140 not out, his maiden century after ten years. As usual John Hampshire summed it up, 'For you to get a 100, Leady, it's clear now that you need to bat on two wickets.'

In 1976 we should have beaten the West Indians at Abbeydale, Sheffield. Yorkshire were without Boycott, but Chris Old (7 for 42 and 45) was in tremendous form and the county needed 109 to win on the last morning.

Unfortunately Barrie Leadbeater (again) had turned his car over on the way home the previous evening and was in hospital.

15

With his fine technique Yorkshire might have just done it: the remaining ten men were bowled out for 90.

Combined Universities beat Yorkshire at Barnsley that year, a terrible humiliation and a result that went round the world. No excuses: we were poor tactically and technically. But may I remind you of some of the players in that 'schoolboy' team? Chris Tavaré, Paul Parker, Peter Roebuck and Vic Marks.

Mike 'Noddy' Bore was soon to leave us for Notts, but not before he added to the quality of life in the Yorkshire dressing room. His captain Geoff Boycott had batted right through an innings against Notts at Bradford and was 129 not out when joined by last man Bore.

Soon a merry little stand had progressed. Noddy had reached 37 not out and another batting point was in reach, when he ran the captain out. In the convulsed dressing room it was suggested that he was trying to steal the bowling.

There was a similar situation at Edgbaston, where Boycott had batted through against Warwickshire, but five runs were still needed to avoid a follow-on when last man Bore, to quote the Birmingham Post, 'came to the wicket with a string of ducks long enough to start a poultry farm'.

There was an earnest consultation in mid-wicket and Bore was no doubt instructed to play out the over carefully so that the captain could steer Yorkshire to safety. Mike nodded, walked back to his crease, took guard, and then whacked Lance Gibbs straight over the stand for six, almost giving Boycott a thrombosis.

Soon afterwards, Boycott returned to the England side to reach his hundredth 100. The 1977 season was to finish with strong rumours that I would be the England reserve wicket-keeper on the winter tour of Pakistan and New Zealand. . .

But they turned out only to be rumours. Not for the first time Paul Downton was chosen as England's reserve wicket-keeper ahead of me. I had to swallow my disappointment and wish him well.

Meanwhile, inside Yorkshire, events on the cricket field were turning into political issues. At Northampton Geoff Boycott as captain took a long time over a century: two batsmen who followed him, John Hampshire and Colin Johnson, refused to take risks in the few remaining overs to the mandatory hundred, so batting bonus points were lost.

The Press raised a storm, suggesting a deliberate 'go-slow', a mutiny even. I was angry at what was happening and refused to pad up. Committee members were there and Boycott and Hampshire were ordered to appear to explain. The committee, as always at that time, tried to steer the middle course, not blaming anyone nor censoring anyone. As a result, each side was able to take home their quarrel for their followers to incorporate in the holy writ of argument. Yorkshire was slowly becoming two camps armed with lawyers.

The Northampton 'go-slow', now almost buried in history, did lead to a sequence of events that not only overturned the committee but also brought me to a captaincy that I wanted, but never expected. Ray Illingworth returned from Leicestershire as Yorkshire's manager, Boycott lost the captaincy to John Hampshire and the Boycott supporters, the Reform Group, sprang to life again with a series of angry meetings that marked the start of a political campaign.

Dissensions ran through the team. John Hampshire, the new captain, seemed to believe that only new success would reunite the side. I remember there were some very hard words over a dropped catch, between Bill Athey and Chris Old at Trent Bridge. Significantly, all three players I have mentioned in this paragraph are now with other counties.

Nor was it possible for Yorkshire to gain new successes easily. Boycott was now regularly playing for the England team while Old, Athey and I were 'fringe' members. This meant that Hampshire rarely had a settled side under his control.

Yorkshire had a big representation in the Centenary Test in 1978: Boycott, Athey, Old and I were all chosen. The occasion, the crowd, and the atmosphere all made it one of the great experiences of my life. A packed house at Lord's, a match that was going into history – the whole affair was enough to make the hairs stand out on the back of my neck.

These were many memorable moments: Chris Old smiting Ray

17

Bright into the Tavern to save a follow-on by England; Kim Hughes charging Old and hitting him straight back onto the top tier of the pavilion, an exhilarating shot; England fielding every day of the Test match; my birthday and wedding anniversary both taking place during that match. But it wasn't all happiness. Gail had a fur coat stolen, along with my wallet containing match expenses, from the hotel room.

Alan Knott hadn't been getting too many runs in the Test series so I was restored to the England side for the fifth Test against West Indies at Leeds. There was no play on the first day because of rain and when England were sent in to bat the sky was overcast and the pitch looked green, just right in fact for one or more of Holding, Croft, Garner and Marshall. When I went in to bat, to join Botham, England were 59-6 and I was very pleased and proud to make 40 before I was lbw to Marshall. I remember hitting Michael Holding for four consecutive fours: I twice cut him over gully, next I clipped him through midwicket for an all-run four and then I drove him through mid-off for four. Need I add that I was ducking the next one?

England were bowled out for 143 and that night Old ran in from the Football End and Greenidge nicked him. At that time Botham was standing very wide at second slip which meant, in turn, that Gooch, at first slip, was also standing wide. I should have realized that, but didn't, and the chance went begging, for I left the ball and it flew through the gap. I can't blame anyone but myself.

There was a tremendous Prudential match at Lord's, one of the finest one-day games I've ever enjoyed. I'm convinced that I caught Desmond Haynes, off Old, very early on, but the decision wasn't given and he went on to make 50 in their total of 235-9. Boycott and Peter Willey gave England a fine start of 135, then we lost wickets trying to score quickly and the match ended in a tremendous scramble. Botham batted beautifully to get England home by three wickets, with three balls to spare.

My England call did come, that following winter, when Roger Tolchard was injured in Australia and I flew out as a replacement. I made my debut in Tasmania, as a substitute fielder, and my first

18

move in overseas cricket was to fling the ball in at the stumps and hit an umpire on the way.

Hampshire was playing for Tasmania at the time and Boycott was in the England team. This situation reminded me of a story of the great days of exploration in Africa, when both the Army and the Royal Navy wanted to be able to claim to be the first across the continent. One started in the east, the other in the west; the two camel trains meeting somewhere in the middle of the Sahara. Do you know what they said, as they saluted each other and passed on? 'Good morning.'

I was a full member of the party for the next Australian tour, 1979-80, when both Graham Stevenson and I were selected for what was as much a triangular one-day series against Australia and West Indies as a proper Test tour. This was the outcome of the Australian Board's peace treaty with the Packer organization World Series Cricket.

The most amazing finish in Australia was under lights at Sydney, when England lost wickets so quickly that the game appeared over. With eight wickets gone, England needed 35 in 6 overs when Stevenson walked out to join me. He had bowled well, taking 4 for 33 and getting a fifth wicket with a run-out from a direct throw.

The ground was electric. The Hill was all keyed up to shout Australia home and I know that up in the Press Box half a dozen stories had already been written celebrating Australia's victory.

Jeff Thomson was all geared up to bowl to Graham, who is never the bravest against really fast bowling. As he walked in, Graham reflected to Ian Chappell, not the most communicative of Australians, 'It's a nice night for it, isn't it?' Chappell, chewing, gave him a glance that suggested he wasn't worth answering.

The first ball from Thomson was vicious. It was fast, short and cutting back, and almost sliced Stevo in half, it tucked him up so much. 'Can you see it?' I called out to him, knowing Graham had never batted under lights before.

'I'm alreet, lad,' he called back. And he was. Never having seen him bat before, the Australians made the very grave error of putting the ball up to him on and outside his off-stump, from where he despatched it with great regularity through and sometimes over an

19

arc between extra cover and long off. When he smacked Thommo straight for six, you have never heard a cricket ground go so quiet so suddenly.

He finished 28 not out, won the match. But, incredibly, Dennis Lillee, 4 for 12 and 0, was man of the match. Why? Because everything was geared to Channel Nine TV and they demanded that the Man of the Match be nominated thirty minutes before the end!

On 14 January 1981, I left for West Indies, as, for the first time, England's senior wicket-keeper. But I had already been told, 'You may be going out as number one, but you'll come back as number two.' Paul Downton had preceded me on one tour, to Pakistan and New Zealand, and he was now travelling as my deputy, both of us serving under Ian Botham as captain and Bob Willis as vice captain. As a tour it wasn't one of the happiest periods of my life.

It began badly on a terrible pitch in Trinidad, where Geoff Dujon got 100. I missed stumping him twice and, deservedly, got a terrible rollicking. I did point out that I had come straight from England, that the surface was concrete, hard and bumpy, and that I needed time to acclimatize. Furthermore I told the captain that 'in situations like this, when people are down, it's up to you to lift them and motivate them'. In turn, he argued that there was no better motivation than playing cricket for your country. I was nightwatchman and I knew what was certain to happen: it did, I was lbw second ball, for nought and that just about summed up my first day of cricket in West Indies.

We went off to St Vincent for a one-day international on another dry, bumpy surface. This time England took precautions: Kenny Barrington knew I was down, so he took me out with a couple of spinners, and batted for a couple of hours to give me practice. It helped. I stumped Andy Roberts down the leg-side, off Graham Gooch, and felt much better for it.

Back to Trinidad, this time for the first Test match, where I contracted a severe case of athlete's foot and couldn't play in the island match preceding the Test. When I got into the nets again, Ian Botham walked up to say I wouldn't be playing in the Test.

He said that the selectors felt that as Paul Downton had become accustomed to the Port of Spain pitch, it was wiser to keep him in the side to meet the full strength of West Indies. My own feeling was that the explanation was just an excuse to drop me.

Full credit to Paul, who played well. I had no axe to grind against him and, looking back, I can now see that suspicions that the captain and selectors wanted me out of the side were not helping my form nor my enjoyment of the tour.

After Trinidad we went on to beautiful Guyana, where Graham Dilley and I had to share a room that wasn't big enough for a single bed. It rained and it rained. We eventually flew off, by army helicopter, to play a one-day game in Berbice. When we flew back to the army barracks, we found the Press all assembled: Robin Jackman, flown out as a replacement, had been barred by the government because of his South African connections.

That meant no Test match in Guyana and a hasty evacuation to Barbados, where we picked up the rest of a tour now badly shaken by politics. And if all that wasn't enough we were then to lose the much-loved Kenny Barrington to a heart attack while in Bridgetown: I miss him still.

The return to Barbados was like approaching paradise, such was the feeling of escape. I played in the Test match and that was to be my last Test: again, it was a difficult pitch to keep on. I didn't shine, but I had the feeling that everyone, particularly in the Press, had made up their minds that they wanted Paul Downton in the side and it would have needed a superhuman performance to have made the slightest difference. Michael Holding bowled some of the quickest overs I've ever seen, and England lost the match to go 2-0 down.

Ian Botham then flew off to Viv Richards' wedding in Antigua, while the team, under new vice captain Geoff Miller, took on Montserrat. Botham left instructions that Paul was to keep in the first innings and myself in the second. Then, just before the match, I was told that I wouldn't be keeping at all, I would play as a batsman. I said to Dusty (Miller): 'I know this means that the decision has already been taken that I am not to play in the Antigua Test.'

Not that Montserrat didn't have its moments. Geoff Boycott got one of the worst lbw decisions I've ever seen, and when he got back to the dressing room his mood can be imagined. Someone offered him a glass of water and he snapped, 'I don't want any . . . glass of water' and threw it out of the dressing-room window. Unfortunately the water flew all over a spectator who, furious, ran to the boundary wall, picked up a whitewashed brick, and returned, threatening to flatten whoever it was who had splashed him. He also happened to be a plain-clothes policeman.

So we then had a large black man with a white brick being restrained from demolishing England's elder statesman batsman by his uniformed colleague. For all we knew there might have been only two policemen on the entire island. The situation was stuff of which farces are made.

England then returned to our original landing place, Antigua, where we had to face the bowling, in the nets, of a very quick sixteen-year-old called George Ferris and where the dressing-room attendant was a lad named Richie Richardson. The Test match pitch was so hard that it made a clinking sound if touched with metal. I was nominated twelfth man (fielding) and did duty through the Test and did not, as is the usual custom on tour, share it with the other members of the tour party who weren't playing. West Indies won the toss for the first Test match ever played in Antigua and all went according to plan for them. Viv Richards, in his home town, hit twelve boundaries in his first 52 runs. Boycott and Willey both scored centuries and England achieved a respectable draw.

Jamaica, the last stop, greeted us with an armed escort that was to stay with us right through the final days of the tour. There are still many people who say that Holding's opening over to Boycott in Barbados was the fastest they'd ever seen. I put Holding's bowling on the second morning of the Jamaica Test even quicker and more hostile. He was lightning that morning, pushing off the boundary wall. Michael told me the pitch would be slow the first day, quicker the second, at its quickest on the third day and then slow down again: and that's exactly what happened. Again, thanks to Graham Gooch and David Gower, England emerged with an honourable draw, although we had to be a little grateful to the surface.

22

The storming of the Winter Palace. (Above) The old régime at bay. The scene in the Conference Centre, Harrogate, on 21 January. (Below) The defeated, the committee members who lost their seats in the landslide. From left to right: Freddie Trueman, Billy Sutcliffe, Desmond Bailey, Ronnie Burnet

In the firing line. From left to right: Julian Vallance, Ronnie Burnet, Michael Crawford, Norman Yardley

The committee rebels: Reg Kirk (left) and Peter Charles represented the pro-Boycott forces inside the old committee

Man in the middle: Yorkshire secretary Joe Lister

The face of triumph. From left to right: Reg Kirk, Sid Fielden,
Peter Charles, Peter Briggs

The rejected: Ronnie Burnet, a former captain who took Yorkshire to the championship, knows that the vote has been lost

Sid Fielden (left) and Geoff Boycott arrive at a press conference in Wakefield after the victory vote

Below: Geoff Boycott reads his statement. Beside him is Tony Vann, secretary of the rebel group

Me at the wicket as the new Yorkshire captain

When Illy first arrived back in Yorkshire in 1978, no one quite knew what to expect. Only Hampshire and Boycott remembered him as a Yorkshire player and Boycs, having lost his mother and the captaincy in the same week, was not too communicative. A lot of people decided that the timing was deliberate, but not even a Yorkshire Committee could think up something as evil as that.

But the question everyone in Yorkshire had asked about Illy was: had he arrived to get rid of Boycott? That begs another question: could Illy have worked with Boycott as captain? Boycott, don't forget, had to mould together a young side: Lumb, Carrick, Stevenson, Cooper, Sidebottom, Athey, Love and me. Illy told us he was keeping his registration but that he wasn't intending to play again. Within weeks Berger Paints came with a strong sponsorship of Yorkshire cricket and Illy was instrumental in that.

But I got on well with Illy at that time, travelling with him quite a lot. The truth is that the minnows in the team, of whom I was one, had no idea of the in-fighting that was already starting behind the scenes. It's obvious now that even then things were being said about players and management that were to cause the great upheavals. I'm not blaming Illy, or anyone else for that matter, for what happened: it was a culmination of many events and incidents.

My bust-up with Illy came over the appointment of Neil Hartley as vice captain in 1981. Neil was uncapped and very junior to me and to several others in the side, and his appointment was tantamount to Illy saying that he didn't rate me or any other of the capped players as a possible captain of Yorkshire. And that hurt.

We went to the nets one Tuesday morning at Headingley when Chris Old was injured. I had put my bags down in the dressing room when Illy called me into his office and said, 'I've got something to tell you. I know you won't approve, but I'm making Neil Hartley captain at Scarborough tomorrow. I think he'll do a good job.'

He added 'You won't agree with this, I know, but I think it's best for the club.' I flared up, 'What have I done wrong?' He murmured something about the wicket-keeper's job.

Still furious, I replied, 'I don't agree with that. And you can stick your nets.' And I stormed out. I didn't travel through to

Scarborough that night, as usual, but left it until the following morning. Stevenson and Sidebottom were running a book. They didn't expect me to turn up at all.

They should have known that I'm not the kind to run away. Yorkshire were playing Warwickshire, and during the game Willie Hogg turned to Hartley and me and asked, 'What's the matter with you two? Aren't you speaking?' Willie thought he was joking but he had in fact spotted the truth of the situation. Neil felt more embarrassed than anything, particularly at the headline stories about an uncapped player leading Yorkshire.

I scored 60-odd runs and that night, unintentionally, I found myself in the cocktail bar, a famous Scarborough establishment known as Hughie's, at the Royal Hotel, along with Illy. I said to him, 'I'm bloody upset you know.'

He replied: 'Well, I know that.'

I then said, 'Why didn't I get a chance to captain the side? There has to be something wrong. I think I deserve a chance.'

Illy replied, 'Just because you've played all these years, you don't have a divine right to captain the side.'

I came back, 'I know I didn't have any divine rights. I just think I should have been given a chance. You've kicked me in the teeth.'

It's at this point that the story soars off into the stratosphere. I'm supposed to have come back at Illy and made allegations about his family. He's supposed to have effed and blinded and told me that if I didn't like it, then I could resign and take Geoff Boycott with me.

So, let's have the record straight. I made no remarks about Ray Illingworth's family. He did not swear at me or suggest that either I or Boycott should resign.

I've been told since that the Yorkshire Club's 'in-depth' inquiry took evidence from the barman at the Royal and from club members present. As one of the participants, I shall stick to my version of what happened.

The 1982 season began unhappily. My father died at the start of the year, which was ironically to be my benefit. The Yorkshire dressing room was far from settled and we had an upheaval halfway through the summer when Old lost the captaincy and Illy took *over. However, after I'd scored 77 against Northants I perked up a little.*

We did have a remarkable match at Edgbaston, where Yorkshire first bowled Warwickshire out for 159 on a poor surface. We were 91-7 and 143 for 9 when Boycott and Stevenson came together to score 149 for the last wicket to beat the Lord Hawke-David Hunter record. This was another unbelievable innings by Graham who said he had got fed up with Boycott always bending his ear, telling him what to do, telling him to concentrate, so he retaliated with a typical but risky Stevenson innings of 115 not out.

Late in June Illy took over as captain, against Essex at Ilford. C.M. Old would never claim to be the best captain in the world but he did try very hard and I would never criticize him for lack of effort. Over the years he had collected many critics, particularly over his fitness, and people called him a hypochondriac. He didn't do himself justice with his own play because he was a much better cricketer than many people think. I was interested to see that Mike Brearley had written that Chilly was only a gene's difference between a very good and a great cricketer, and that is very true. In ability, particularly in English conditions, he was only a shade behind such players as Botham, Imran Khan, Hadlee and Kapil Dev.

He lost the captaincy after Yorkshire had played in his home town of Middlesbrough. Illy had told me a few times that he contemplated playing again. What may have started him thinking on those lines was the match against Scotland the previous year when Old, for his own reasons, did something totally different from what had been planned overnight and Illy went berserk at lunchtime.

So Illingworth resumed as captain with Boycott, who captained the side occasionally, playing under him. The strange thing was that, whatever was being said or written off the field by partisans of both sides, Illingworth and Boycott got on perfectly well once on the field. You would never have guessed there was the slightest animosity between them. There is no doubt that their respect for each other as cricketers was total and I have to wonder sometimes if the team had been left alone whether all would not have been resolved peacefully.

25

Let's have something else for the record: there was no trouble in the dressing room at this time. Of course, the odd hard word was exchanged, but that's normal and inevitable when everyone has been keyed up and a match has been won or lost. But there were none of the slanging matches I've heard about so much outside, certainly not between Illy and G.B.

My benefit year got a splendid boost in the Derbyshire match at Scarborough. I equalled the world record of seven catches in the first innings, and the match record with eleven in all. Better still, Yorkshire won the game by six wickets. We almost finished with another win at the Oval where Surrey were hanging on at 294-8. In the second innings Sylvester Clarke bowled in sand shoes and off three paces, sending the ball through amazingly quickly.

We had an encouraging Nat-West summer, beating Worcestershire with three balls to spare, a magnificent win, then beating Essex on a steamy humid morning (10.30 a.m. starts that year) at Leeds. Essex were 51-9, recovered to 132, but the pitch was difficult and we lost Boycott for 14, though Moxon was in fine form. Down came a terrific thunderstorm and when it cleared the ground was under water.

Keith Fletcher and Essex then took a very sporting and realistic decision. Yorkshire needed only another 20 runs, and even if it rained again, Essex would lose on the scoring faster rate. So, to save Essex all the expense of another overnight stay in Leeds, play was resumed in totally farcical conditions.

Yorkshire now thought they had a chance of the final, but the whole campaign collapsed in the semi-final against Warwickshire at Edgbaston. We lost the toss, had to bat first on a wicket that was still drying out and made 216 for 9; after that the pitch settled down, the ball stopped seaming and Warwickshire won comfortably.

The summer of 1983 has to be remembered chiefly for Yorkshire's winning of the John Player League Championship. I know the legend has got about that we won it because of the weather. To answer this charge I would merely point to the record: won ten, lost three, no result three.

The League was, in fact, won by fielding first most of the time. We lost to Somerset batting first, to Notts batting first and, although we lost to Glamorgan batting second, Boycott had been left out of the side.

Amid all this we had some superb victories, among them Hampshire at Middlesbrough and Derbyshire at Bradford. In the match against Derbyshire Billy Athey batted with one arm after being injured in a car smash; Simon Dennis lifted Ole Mortensen straight into the pavilion for six to win that one. I also remember that match for three stumpings – in a Sunday match!

But now let us look at the other side of the coin. Yorkshire failed to qualify for the knock-out stages in the Benson & Hedges competition and fell to Northants in the Nat-West Cup. Above all, this was Yorkshire's worst-ever season in the competition we once dominated: the county championship. We won only one game and, although our friends have pointed out that five of the seventeen matches that were drawn were victories in all but name, all I can reply to that is to ask whoever remembers the names of beaten semi-finalists? Essex, the champions, also lost only five matches but that was the only comparison between our record and theirs.

Inconsistency was our main enemy: only three batsmen, Boycott, Bairstow and Love, scored 1,000. Moxon, Sharpe and Lumb all spent long periods in the second team. We did see Ashley Metcalfe make a brilliant debut against Notts, and there was promise of much cricket to come from Ian Swallow, Paul Booth and Stuart Fletcher. Simon Dennis was capped and did exceptionally well.

The storms began to gather at Cheltenham, where Boycott was reported by Illingworth for slow scoring. I wasn't privy to any of the discussions that went on, but I do believe there was some kind of breakdown in communications and that Boycott was in some confusion as to what his orders were supposed to be. It also has to be said that, with his vast experience, he should have had a good idea of what was needed without having to be told. To be fair to Boycott he did try to move the score along and was in fact lucky to escape being stumped, twice.

Whatever happened, and whoever was to blame, the fact is we

27

had another political incident on our hands when something had happened that should never have got beyond the doors of the dressing room. After that, the battle lines were drawn. Boycott's supporters went for Illy and Illy's friends attacked Boycott. The committee seemed to manage to infuriate both factions by offering Boycott a testimonial in 1984, and then sacking him.

By October I'd got the whisper that I was to be appointed captain. I was pleased and proud as any Yorkshireman would have been. But I still couldn't see the logic of the Boycott situation: surely it made more sense to give Boycott another contract and have him in the side, rather than sack him and then allow him to take collections for his benefit on Yorkshire grounds?

I was soon sick to the teeth with the whole business. I cringed when I saw the club tearing itself apart: Freddie Trueman, saying on television that Boycott should have been sacked ten years before; then Bob Slicer, a leading Boycott supporter, telling the rebel group Yorkshire Members 1984, 'You don't sack the top of the bill when the rest of the show is rubbish.' That hurt, and I got an apology from Mr Slicer.

Boycott rang me a couple of times and was clearly very upset about being sacked. He also asked me one or two other things and it was clear, from what was coming from the committee, that both sides were trying to use me and I resented that. The last thing I wanted was to take sides over an argument that was ripping my club apart.

Came the elections, the old committee was overthrown (it was suggested during the election that I should stand for one of the Bradford seats!) and G.B. sailed triumphantly back, reinstated as a player and a committeeman for Wakefield.

I had my own problems. I was working in a Bradford store that winter when I was approached by a member, who congratulated me on the captaincy, wished me luck and left, saying over his shoulder, 'One last thing. Watch your back.'

Saturday, 28 April–Tuesday, 1 May

Somerset v Yorkshire
at Taunton

Yorkshire beat Somerset by 3 wickets

My first match as captain was a tense moment for the Yorkshire team and for me. We had to play Somerset at Taunton in a championship match, the first under the new sponsors, Britannic Assurance; but it wasn't that fact that drew the media to Taunton like bees converging on pollen. There were so many questions about the match. Ian Botham's reign as Somerset captain had begun in controversy after he had flown home early from England's winter tour of Pakistan to have a knee operation and to fight off allegations about drug taking. How would Botham play? How would Somerset play without their two West Indian superstars, Viv Richards and Joel Garner, called up for the 1984 West Indies tour of England? How would Martin Crowe, the young New Zealander signed by Somerset for a year to help fill the gap, fare?

Just as intriguing were questions of how Yorkshire would fare under David Bairstow, and how Boycott would appear, and play, after first being sacked and then triumphing in the committee room?

Fleet Street was there in force, along with two television channels and Yorkshire's regular press corps of John

Callaghan, *Yorkshire Evening Post*, David Warner, *Telegraph and Argus, Bradford*, David Hopps, *Yorkshire Post*, and Martin Searby.

Of course I was nervous. Just before breakfast in the County Hotel, Taunton, I received a telephone call from Australia. Terry Brindle, the former *Yorkshire Post* correspondent and now a freelance in Sydney, an old friend of mine and the writer who helped Geoff Boycott with all his books, rang to wish us all good luck, a heartwarming gesture that eased the tension a little. I breakfasted with Richard Lumb and Martyn Moxon and got to the ground early because I had arranged to see Ted Lester there to take a good look at the pitch.

Ted, a very fine free-scoring Yorkshire batsman of the 1950s – he once scored two centuries in the same Roses match; no mean feat – has been the county scorer for many years. I value his judgement greatly, both his estimation of playing conditions and of players. Boycott drove me to the ground, missed the right turn, couldn't find his way back, so we were late. If Boycs didn't carry a map in his car, he wouldn't be able to find his way home.

The pitch looked green, contained a fair amount of moisture and appeared to have a good deal more bounce and pace than anything we had seen in our month of practice at Headingley. After a discussion with Ted, I decided that if I won the toss I would have to field; I couldn't take the risk of exposing our batsmen to a surface that might well be at its liveliest in the first two hours.

So when I won the toss and sent in Somerset, who scored 246 without losing a wicket and eventually declared at 298-5, I had some terrible stick from the Sunday papers. The implication was that as a new captain I was a total idiot. Allow me to let those clever Sunday writers into a secret: if Botham had won the toss, he would have sent in Yorkshire.

I went back to the dressing room to warn our players, 'This isn't a pitch on which we'll get them out for 100, so I don't want anybody busting a gut. If we bowl well and take our chances we might have them out for 200.'

30

Somerset went in to bat and Peter Roebuck and Julian Wyatt must have played and missed on an average about three times an over. Wyatt nicked a ball just short of Boycott at second slip, which the *Sunday Mirror* described as a missed chance. Nonsense! Boycott caught the ball cleanly, so how could it be a missed chance?

I now know that the biggest mistake I made at Taunton was to take Graham Stevenson. I have the greatest respect for his ability: he can be a very good bowler and a fine all-round cricketer, but he had been complaining of pressure on his hip all through April. And although the hamstring injury that put him out of the match didn't occur until after the game had started, I realize I should have left him behind.

I know that I was on edge all that Saturday. The television interviews hadn't helped. One interviewer began by saying that Yorkshire had a disastrous year in 1983. I had to interrupt him to point out that Yorkshire were the John Player League champions. Not content with that, he followed up with another question, 'How is your relationship with last year's captain, Geoff Boycott?' I had to point out that Ray Illingworth was last year's captain. It was nice to get a few words of congratulation from some Somerset members, who were listening. I appreciated, too, the compliments from the Somerset Committee on Yorkshire's dress and deportment.

Meanwhile on the field Arnie Sidebottom, who has a heart as big as a mountain, was bowling without any luck at all. Roebuck might have been run out had not Stevenson fumbled a return. Wyatt might have been run out had not Carrick's return hit a foothold, the ball bouncing out of my reach. The ball was constantly being edged just wide of the slips.

And then, after a particularly frustrating day, Boycott went in to hook Botham for four. I was pleased about that. He was being positive. But no one, not even me, would then try to hook the penultimate ball of the day as he did, getting caught on the boundary for six. It showed a lack of responsibility and was a disgraceful performance for a man who has been in the game for twenty-three years.

I know why Geoff did it. Botham was the bowler and it was a personal challenge. It was a shot of defiance, an attempt to prove he was bigger than Botham, and it made for pathetic cricket. We could have been in serious trouble, and might have followed on, had Botham not been too proud to post a third man. As it was we made 242 and were able to study the Botham captaincy at first hand. He was very much in charge, never appearing to consult the previous year's captain, Brian Rose.

We certainly expected him to bowl more overs. The obvious explanation was that he wasn't fully fit. If that were true, then he shouldn't have played. A fully-fit Botham should have personally put us under more pressure, instead of passing the buck to Davis, Dredge and Crowe.

We were a bowler short, Stevenson having broken down, when Somerset batted again. This may explain why they seemed to have a slightly contemptuous attitude towards Yorkshire, even why they gave us the second declaration, leaving us to get 306 in 78 overs.

By tea we were 82-1 and were able to reassess the situation. We had to wake Arnie up for the Discussion. Arnie is a great sleeper. Boycott thought a win was out of the question. He said it was difficult to bat out there. I thought about this and then told Stevenson, our big hitter, to get padded up because I was determined, even if a win proved impossible, to make a token effort.

Before the restart Boycott asked, 'Well, how are we going to play?'

I replied, 'Just bat. Try to be positive and we'll see what happens.'

I could sense that the rest of the dressing room wanted to have a go, even if we lost, although I wasn't at all happy at the thought of losing my first match as captain.

But Lumb, Carrick, Love were all indicating that they thought we had to make the attempt. Boycott cannot bear to fail personally. That's why he always reduces risks to the minimum. But to be fair he went out after tea and played well. Before Lumb was out there was a good deal of discussion as to who should go in next. At least Carrick was decisive. He said I should be the one. I pondered for five minutes and then said, 'Right, I'm going in.' There was a fair amount of colourful writing the following morning about my arriving at the crease and giving Boycott a good finger-wagging; the implication being that I'd told him to get a move on.

Not true. All I said was, 'Keep going, Boycs. If you get a 100 we'll win this match.'

He replied, 'Don't go mad. Play for the first 20 then see how it goes.'

That was sound advice. The first ball was a full toss, so I hit it for four. Two balls later I got a bouncer, which I hooked for four. Another two balls and I got a half-volley that I drove through extra cover for four.

Boycott growled, 'I told you to play for 20.'

I shot back, 'I can't bloody help it. If they bowl rubbish I'll have to hit it.'

That burst gave the innings momentum. I have noticed before that I can, by example, light a fuse under Geoffrey Boycott. He, too, started to play shots and was then out, unluckily. I signalled for Jim Love to come in next – we got that right, too – and had to wait, after an exciting win by three wickets with eleven balls to spare, to hear what happened in the dressing room.

The lads know Boycott all too well to say too much to him when he's out. This time Stevenson broke the ice by saying, 'Well, what do you think?' meaning, 'How are we doing?'

Boycott snapped 'It's nowt to do with me. I'm not the captain.'

Boycott then thawed a little, pointing out how difficult it was to score against Vic Marks, and adding, 'He always knows what he's doing and where the ball is going, not like some I could mention', a remark that had Stevenson quietly kicking Carrick at the back of the dressing room.

At that moment I went down the track to hit Marks over

long off for six, whereupon Stevenson quickly added, 'Aye, and he knew where that one was going, too.' That broke the ice, Boycott laughed, got caught up in the spirit of the chase and began organizing the batting order.

He enjoyed the victory as much as anyone and I knew that I needed to convince him that he was wanted in the team, that his vast ability was needed, that he had a new contract and another after that if he really wanted it and that there was nothing left for him to prove or to worry about. I had to convince him that he was safe in Yorkshire with a seat on the committee, and that the odd failure in the course of the season wouldn't make a scrap of difference to how we or the Yorkshire public regarded him.

Out at the wicket, I'd felt confident of winning from the moment I middled the first ball. Jim Love played well at the other end, Kevin Sharp and Arnie made valuable contributions and finally Stevenson, wearing white inner batting gloves to stop him biting his nails, went in to finish them off.

I left thinking that Ian Botham needed to lose a dozen pounds. He wasn't half the bowler we expected to face. We had turned the tables on the critics and I have to add that by far the best account of what happened in the match, a reporting of the cricket and not a half-dozen total irrelevancies, came from Somerset's own local leading cricket writer, Eric Hill.

Leicestershire v Yorkshire
at Headingley

Yorkshire beat Leicestershire by 7 wickets

We returned North to open our Benson & Hedges zonal matches by defeating Leicestershire by seven wickets at Headingley. But then, on the Sunday at Bradford, we came to earth with a bump by losing our first John Player League match, as champions, to Worcestershire by 31 runs. It wasn't the happiest of weekends for Geoff Boycott and he annoyed me by his attitude.

He was out cheaply against Leicestershire, came back to the dressing room, kicked Stuart Fletcher's bag, blamed the pitch, swore at 'having to play on a pitch like that' and then, when we'd won, left without saying a word.

He grumbled something about, 'I'm under so much pressure.'

I replied, 'If people weren't behind you, you would not be out on this field today.'

My expression must have betrayed my feelings as he left.

However, let's talk about the good things. I was uncertain whether to play Stuart Fletcher. He is only nineteen and runs can be so tight in one-day games that one loose over can lose the match. My faith in him was confirmed by Peter Willey, captain of a Leicestershire team

35

severely hit by injuries and illness (no David Gower, Paddy Clift or George Ferris). Said Peter, a Geordie who never wastes a word, 'He's a good bowler, that lad.' And when I was talking over the match with the Leicestershire lads afterwards, Ken Higgs, now their coach and a fine bowler in his time, added, 'Keep faith with the lad. Back his ability. Encourage him.'

Fletcher, Kevin Sharp and Phil Carrick all did well against Leicestershire and I also have to mention Steve Oldham's contribution. Bringing him home has been a very wise move.

We had one very good laugh out on the field at Headingley. One of the umpires was Barrie Leadbeater, often Boycott's opening partner on some highly dramatic occasions in the 1970s. Now he was the man to decide, perhaps, the fate of Geoff's next innings. Grinned 'Leady', 'Boycs spoke to me more often out on the field today than he did in the entire ten years I played with him.' As an umpire Leadbeater did especially well. He certainly got high marks from me.

Yorkshire v Worcestershire
at Bradford

Worcestershire beat Yorkshire by 31 runs

We were doing so well against Worcestershire on Sunday, too, when the wheels fell off. Perhaps a defeat, at this stage of the season, was no bad thing. Stuart again did well, bowling his 8 overs for 25 and taking a wicket. At 63-0, off 17 overs needing 174 to win, Yorkshire should have cantered home instead of being bowled out, in 38 overs, for 142. Two things turned the match: Yorkshire conceded 30 extras, virtually the margin between the teams, 18 leg byes, 10 wides and a no-ball. That must stop.

And Martyn Moxon, the first wicket to fall, was dismissed through an astonishing catch by David Humphries. He took off down the leg-side, realized that the ball would pass the other side of him, flung out his right hand and the ball stuck. A fantastic catch, but a lucky one.

I made my mind up about two moves over this weekend. I intended to press for a county cap for Martyn Moxon. His place as opening batsman is assured as long as he wants it, he has a ton of ability and if he doesn't play for England this coming 1984 summer, then he must have an outstanding chance of touring India in the winter. There is no point in delaying his Yorkshire cap.

I've also decided that I will not rush Graham Stevenson back into the side. He will now have to prove his fitness in the second team, before being brought back. Good friend though he is, Graham has to realize that he does not have an automatic place in the team.

I wasn't too amused by the attitude of a member of the committee either. Wanting a bat signed by the Worcestershire team on the Sunday, by mistake he came into our dressing room, saying, 'Well played!' When he discovered that he was with the defeated, he just retreated. No word of apology. No 'Hard luck'.

Wednesday, 9 May–Friday, 11 May

Nottinghamshire v Yorkshire
at Headingley

Yorkshire beat Nottinghamshire by 6 runs

Considerable forethought had gone into our next championship match, against Notts at Headingley. Although Clive Rice suffered a back injury in 1983, he and Richard Hadlee remained the most feared and respected opening attack in county cricket and there are some good judges who rate Hadlee the best new-ball bowler in the world. We certainly didn't want to meet them on a green pitch; we were hoping for a pitch that would turn and suit our spinners.

Neil Hartley was upset at not getting in the XI that I chose, and I think he had every right to be. Perhaps he went

38

off to play in the second team feeling that I had a prejudice against him. Far from it, I was very sympathetic but I felt I had to pick the best-balanced side for a three-day game. I wanted Ian Swallow, our young off-spinner, in the team because I have faith in his future. He will become a good cricketer.

I won the toss to make it four wins out of four to date – no captain can ask for more than that – and the sensation of the first innings was Boycott's run out by Derek Randall. There had been a few jokes exchanged between the pair; Boycott taunting Randall with 'You'll never get me out'. Alas, when he did take a real gamble, 'Arkle' did him completely, by a yard.

Had not the weather intervened we would have achieved 400 plus, but there was less than half an hour's play on the second day. Notts batted for an hour on the Friday morning, then declared – I could have enforced a follow-on, but they would then have shut the game down – and we batted again long enough to set them to get 301 in 77 overs. The pitch was firm, the outfield had dried and several in our dressing room thought I'd been over-generous. Notts bat a long way down – Hadlee appears higher in New Zealand's order than he does for Notts – and they had a long time to pace the innings.

But, as usual, I was the supreme optimist. I saw no point in accepting a mediocre draw. We had to entice them into having a go at a target; that was the only way they might give us the opportunity to bowl them out.

When Richard Lumb dropped Rice when he was at 7, my heart sank. 'The bubble's burst,' I thought to myself. I expected Notts to walk away with it. Yet no Yorkshire heads dropped. We kept plugging away and, whatever my inner feelings, I certainly made it plain that I still believed we could win.

And we did. Sidebottom came roaring back to bowl Rice, Boycott caught Randall at slip for the second time in one day – a neat revenge – and with three balls left and seven runs wanted, Simon Dennis bowled the Notts last man,

39

Kevin Cooper. Notts supporters must have wondered why, at 237-7, Rice didn't order his tailenders to play for an honourable draw.

The reason was that with Bruce French hitting two sixes and five fours (55 off 47 balls) a Notts victory was still possible, as long as they kept on going. For my part, I kept the field spread, partly for obvious defensive reasons and partly to encourage the later batsmen to hit out.

Saturday, 12 May

Scotland v Yorkshire
at Perth

Yorkshire beat Scotland by 45 runs

Immediately after that match we had to board a coach to travel to Perth for the Benson & Hedges fixture against Scotland. With two wins from two championship matches we had every reason to celebrate; spirits were high, even though we didn't get into Perth until one o'clock in the morning and the hotel was hardly first class. Boycott and I were then awakened by a barking dog, and he chose to go without breakfast, preferring an extra half hour's sleep before we left for the ground at 9.45.

It was a beautiful setting, alongside the Tay, with free admission for the public, but little thought had been given to the players' facilities. We had to change in a sports centre, four hundred yards away, then march down carrying our gear, to park our bags in a tent. Yes, I know I'll be accused of whinging. The reply is always the same, 'Surely you can put up with a little inconvenience for a one-day game?'

Of course we can. Except that the one-day game for most people present is our umpteenth one-day game of the summer, and the umpteenth occasion that we have put up with poor facilities, and the umpteenth time we have been told, 'Surely you can put up with it for just one day'.

This time Richard Lumb had to be left out. Again I regretted it but I was obliged to go for the all-rounders. We had a mini-collapse, after I'd lost the toss. Boycott made some very uncomplimentary remarks about the pitch; Moxon ran himself out; I was out the first over after lunch. But after that, Jim Love took over to hit the ball a very long way and thoroughly deserved his Gold Award. Sidebottom hit a big six and I was fairly confident that, on a slow pitch, we could tie Scotland down, and so it proved.

The story, as the Press saw it, revolved round the tea interval. I had been notified that under the new rules tea would be taken after 35 overs of the second innings and had planned my bowling accordingly. The umpires, Dickie Bird and John Holder, had not been told of the change – the letters were awaiting them at home – and accordingly took the teams off after 25 overs.

I went off to point out the discrepancy to Dickie, who was also shown a letter from the TCCB to the Scottish Cricket Union. As I saw it the umpires, who are in sole charge, could have decreed that the one tea interval was enough.

Not Dickie. He played safe by having another tea interval after 35 overs, a move that totally mystified the crowd. Many had probably never seen county cricket before and assumed it happened every day, putting it all down as another example of English eccentricity.

More important from our point of view was that we had another two points towards qualifying for the Benson & Hedges quarter-finals. Morale was good despite a delay, on the way home on Sunday morning, caused by the inability of one of the travelling Pressmen to wake up in time. There had been resistance to having the Press sharing the cost of the bus, and a twenty-minute delay didn't improve tempers.

Warwickshire v Yorkshire
at Edgbaston

Warwickshire beat Yorkshire by 7 runs

Arnie Sidebottom's great efforts over the first fortnight of the season caught up with him before the Benson & Hedges fixture against Warwickshire at Edgbaston. A pulled hamstring forced him out of the side, which meant that we went into the match with a very young and inexperienced attack, and paid the price. Nevertheless we only lost after a very gallant effort to get the runs.

Bob Willis returned to the Warwickshire side after recovering from his winter illness. An almost skeletal Willis, pale and thin, but still capable enough of showing our young men how to bowl length and line, even if the old pace wasn't there. Boycott made us smile by declaring, 'I knew he would play in this match. They all want to bowl at me, you know.'

We did a reasonable containing job on Warwickshire's powerful batting until Chris Old came in: we should know what he can do to spinners. He got hold of young Swallow in one very expensive over and along with Ferreira gave Warwickshire a far better total than I had anticipated, but we had ourselves partly to blame. We didn't bowl a good line to either Ferreira or Andy Lloyd and we gave away a good 30 runs in the field. A big topic in our dressing room: why has 'Chilly' Old taken to wearing beads?

Bob Willis then gave his bowling demonstration to our young men, while Boycott didn't seem to know where his stumps were. Fortunately Moxon and Sharp played superbly and put us back into the match before again we fell behind: badly enough this time for me to think it might have cost us the game. In the four overs before tea only two runs were added when 10 to 15 were needed. In effect, we reduced our batting time from 55 overs to 51, a bad tactical error.

Kevin Sharp became involved in running out Jim Love. I batted number five again, but by then we were needing 6-7 runs an over. Then, in the nick of time the hero appeared. Neil Hartley, although obliged to borrow Simon Dennis's bat, played a tremendous knock of 65 not out that rightly brought him the Gold Award. We actually reached a point where we needed 24 off the last two overs and failed by just 7 runs which, considering the mistakes we had made earlier, represented a fine recovery. We were beaten but spirits were good and morale was high. This match went into the records under the heading 'Experience'.

Had either of our all-rounders, Sidebottom or Graham Stevenson, been available, I'm convinced we would have won. We had to pay a price for Edgbaston when our third all-rounder, Neil Hartley, strained his right arm and was knocked out of the following weekend's one-day games.

Yorkshire v Northamptonshire
at Bradford

Yorkshire beat Northamptonshire by 7 wickets

Our final Benson & Hedges zonal game was against Northants at Bradford. We knew that Warwickshire were certain to finish top in our zone, but we had a superior striking rate – wickets per ball bowled – to Northants or Leicestershire which meant, paradoxically, that it was possible for us to lose and still qualify, provided that our rate wasn't overtaken in the process.

The pressure was even greater on George Sharp, Northants' acting captain (Geoff Cook was injured). He had three aims: to win; to take as many Yorkshire wickets as he could; and to lose as few wickets as possible.

Having won the toss, he naturally batted first. Although I'd lost Hartley, I gambled on giving Sidebottom a longer rest because we did have Stevenson fit again, and his own peculiar Ackworth brand of humour was welcomed in the dressing room. I also decided to keep playing young Swallow and he repaid me with two tremendous catches.

We knew what Wayne Larkins could do behind square on the leg-side and made provision accordingly. We didn't know what a big lad from Staffordshire, named Rob Bailey, could do but he soon showed us, hitting six sixes, four of

44

them off Carrick, three of them landing on the roof of the Park Avenue pavilion. Feelings were running high by lunch.

As we came off the field I let fly, 'There's been more bloody chat coming up the steps than there was out in the middle all morning. It's like fielding in a morgue. What encouragement is that to our bowlers?'

I was warmed up by now, 'I haven't lost my temper with you yet this season, but I have now. And if you don't bloody well like it you can lump it.'

The point I was making was that a batsman likes to be encouraged when he comes back to the dressing room. A 'well-played' is worth a lot to him. Similarly bowlers, out on the field, need support, especially from the close field. Middlesex and Worcestershire are two sides that are good at this. If you bowl for Middlesex you must feel like a world-beater every time you turn your arm.

Anyway, it worked. We were twice as sharp in the afternoon and one player confided to me, 'You were right to give us a rollicking. We needed a sharpening up.' Martyn Moxon gave us a handsome spell after lunch and for that I have to thank Boycott, who kept pressing me to bowl 'Froggy'.

I'll explain the nickname. When Martyn first appeared in the dressing room, a strongly-built lad from South Yorkshire, he wore glasses with lenses so thick that the team, with their usual sense of diplomacy, quickly decided he looked like a frog. When he began wearing lenses the origin of the name became lost but lingers on, along with another, 'Ower Both'. That means 'Our Botham' and is a tribute to Martyn's growing all-round prowess.

We needed 252 to defeat Northants and I have to describe Yorkshire's batting that Saturday as fabulous. Boycott's 106 was a reminder of how well he can play. He did relax; he played shots as if he didn't have a care in the world. I realized that if I could get him to play like this all season he would get 2,000 runs in the championship alone, and Yorkshire would have to win something.

Yorkshire v Nottinghamshire
at Hull

Nottinghamshire beat Yorkshire by 19 runs

By Sunday, of course, the world had turned upside down again. On a cold, gloomy rainy day at Hull, Notts, out for revenge, were too experienced for us on a very dodgy pitch. There were holes in the dressing-room floor, the outfield was a disgrace and, not surprisingly, the umpires reported the pitch after Notts had beaten us by 19.

Because I didn't want one of our youngsters exposed to possible ridicule from a 4,000 plus crowd, I sent Phil Carrick down to third man. His comment afterwards was, 'It's the first time I've ever fielded on a ground under repair.'

Ashley Metcalfe, who came into the side because Boycott had strained his right leg on the previous day, did very well in the outfield, taking three catches. I felt a little sorry for the lad. I had him padded up to go in number three if we lost a wicket quickly. In fact, Lumb and Moxin put on 49 and after that I had to shuffle the order in an attempt to keep up the scoring rate, which meant that young Ashley didn't get in to bat until the match was virtually lost.

I was pleased to see that Ashley had been given an early chance to return to the first team, after his century in his debut against Notts in 1983, but he was lucky. The player I really wanted on that Sunday was Philip Robinson, a right-hander from Keighley, who had finished top of the Colts' averages (60.00) the previous summer and who had scored 113 and 55 not out for the second team the previous midweek. Philip was not regarded as a great stylist, but his scoring feats compelled us to give him a chance to move up in class, just to see whether he could continue to add to his mountain of runs. It wasn't until I got to the dressing room that I discovered, due to an administrative mix-up, Philip wasn't even a registered Yorkshire player and his debut had to be delayed.

Richard Lumb produced some bold batting in his first John Player League match for four years and said to me, grinning, as he got back to the dressing room, 'I see I'll have to be careful, Stanley. If I go on playing like this, you'll be wanting me again and I've got used to my Sunday pint and dinner at home!'

Two thoughts on that defeat at Hull. First, as John Player League champions we had been beaten in our opening two matches. I fully expected to hear a few critics say that we had won in 1983 only through Ray Illingworth's spin bowling. I had to grin and bear that, because the hard fact was that Yorkshire hadn't won a JPL match under me.

The second was the consideration of actually playing in Hull. The club itself argues that the attendances justify taking matches there. I'm not so sure. Do they really believe that Yorkshire members in Hull pay their subscriptions just to see one one-day game a year? I can't believe that. I believe that the majority of Hull members see most of their cricket in Leeds and Scarborough, and would firmly support moving the fixture to one of those two grounds. Hull is not properly equipped for first-class cricket and until it is I think Yorkshire should play elsewhere. I doubt if any member of the Yorkshire team would disagree with me.

The defeat by Notts ended the first phase of the season. Yorkshire then had almost a week off before the Roses match against Lancashire and it gave me a chance to take stock.

47

We were in the quarter-finals of the Benson & Hedges competition, drawn away to Sussex at Hove, and second in the Britannic Championship table. The only disappointment was our bottom place in the John Player League but neither of our two defeats was really a bad one. We know where we went wrong, which is important for our education.

In the dressing room there were a lot of plusses. All the batsmen had scored runs, Martyn Moxon was about to get his county cap, and from our successful second XI we had introduced, almost without setbacks, Stuart Fletcher, Ian Swallow and Ashley Metcalfe. Our two strike bowlers, Sidebottom and Stevenson, were fit again and our third all-rounder, Neil Hartley, was in such form that his presence was a threat to virtually anyone in the side.

I'd had a few ups and downs with Geoffrey, but both he and I knew that would happen, and I don't believe either of us felt less about the other as a result. Perhaps the crucial happening of those first three weeks was the lift in spirits that comes from winning.

Saturday, 26 May–Monday, 28 May

Yorkshire v Lancashire
at Headingley

Yorkshire drew with Lancashire

A Roses match is a special trial for any captain, whether it is
his first or twenty-first season in charge. The great
Northern fixture between Yorkshire and Lancashire may
not create as much interest and excitement as it did in the
1920s and 1930s and shortly after the Second World War,
when Bank Holiday attendances of 25,000 upwards were
expected, but there is still a strongly individual feeling
about the match.

The players get along very well. Times have changed
since the two counties only ever met twice a season.
Nowadays there is the annual John Player League match,
plus the possibility of meeting in the other domestic one-
day competitions; so the two dressing rooms are pretty
friendly. The real feuding is only carried on between the
two committees. Neither wants to lose, so captains and
teams tend to be ultra-cautious which, in turn, leads to
many drawn encounters and the perennial accusation that
the fixture is just a bore. I don't think many cricket-lovers in
the North ever find it a bore. If cricket were only about
winning and losing matches, the game would have died a
century ago.

The situation at Leeds on 26 May was that both counties were entering a Roses match with a new captain; John Abrahams and myself. We had made the better start and several Lancashire players were struggling to find form, so that, having won the toss, I was perfectly happy to bat, even though I realized that the pitch would probably help the bowlers. At 14–4 I felt as if the roof had fallen in.

We were without Geoff Boycott, who had a hamstring strain. Three of our batsmen were caught at short square leg, or Boot Hill as we call it. Nobody's fault, just very good bowling on Lancashire's part, making the best of the conditions. I went in and, I thought, played pretty well, achieving 62 before getting myself out to a rather silly shot just before lunch.

After that Yorkshire virtually capitulated at 180 all out. Recalling what was to happen on the following day, Sunday, I have to admit that I was not keeping wicket very well. I wasn't happy with my form – I was batting well enough – and would be hard pressed to explain what was going wrong. No doubt if I had raised the matter, I would have been told that keeping wicket and captaining a team is traditionally one of the game's most demanding jobs.

Anyway, I dropped Graeme Fowler, a gloved catch going down the legside, off Arnie Sidebottom. Arnie is the worst bowler to suffer like that. He is such a competitor that you can almost feel the heartbreak when Arnie has done his job, he's totally beaten the batsmen and then, for reasons known only to God, the ball shaves the stumps or the bails, the keeper or close field drop the catch, the umpire turns down a perfectly valid lbw appeal. Arnie, you might say, suffers for his art.

Arnie apart, I wasn't too happy with the way we bowled, either. The result was that by the end of the day Lancashire were riding high, having assembled their biggest opening stand in Yorkshire since the 1920s. I was furious when I discovered that Simon Dennis, who had been opening the attack with Sidebottom, had taken the field with a swollen ankle. Although it did explain one of our weaknesses, it was something he had concealed from everyone.

That lit the fuse, I went wild when we got back into the dressing room and young Simon got an earful. I pointed out that he had let down the club, the public and his team-mates by his stupidity. I sent him off to see the physiotherapist and told him I didn't want to see him again until he could prove he was fully fit.

Sunday's play was wiped out by rain, but that was the day I learned I had been selected for England's one-day squad in the Texaco Trophy competition; three matches against West Indies. The news came first to me via a rumour from a press photographer. It was then confirmed by the Yorkshire chairman, Reg Kirk, who broke the news to the dressing room and then very kindly sent up three bottles of champagne for a little celebration.

I had seen my name mentioned and knew I was among the candidates but I didn't really expect to be selected because I knew I wasn't keeping well, despite getting an award as wicket-keeper of the month. I knew very well that the award was really for the improvement in Yorkshire's form and I guessed that the selectors wanted me as much for any quick runs that I might be able to contribute as for my keeping.

Before I turned my thoughts to playing for England, we had to finish the match against Lancashire. They put up an amazing and disgraceful performance on the Monday, batting on until any possible hope of a result had gone and, in the process, failing to get maximum batting points. Despite all that was said afterwards about not letting Yorkshire back into the game, the truth had to be that Lancashire were absolutely terrified of losing. They dropped to the bottom of the championship table after this match and fully deserved to be there. If Yorkshire had played that kind of cricket at Old Trafford, the crowd would have been on the pitch. They have that kind of crowd there.

England v West Indies
at Old Trafford, Trent Bridge, Lord's

West Indies beat England by 2 matches to 1

Happy as I was to be reporting to England at Old Trafford on the following Wednesday, I still wanted to see something of Yorkshire, playing Sussex in Sheffield. So, I travelled to Manchester by a roundabout route and remember the day as much as anything for the drive, in gloriously clear weather, across the Pennines. As was agreed before the season's start, the senior professional took over the Yorkshire leadership, and I thought it was a measure of how the club was settling down again that no great fuss was made over the fact that the senior professional was Geoff Boycott.

Old Trafford that Thursday was the setting for what was almost certainly the greatest innings ever played in a one-day match. Viv Richards scored more than all England's batsmen put together and he seemed to know exactly how to do what he intended to do. When England had seven West Indies wickets down, Viv was about 55 and Eldine Baptiste just into double figures. I overheard Viv say to Eldine, as I walked past at the end of an over, 'Come on

Bappo, come on Bappo, it's my day, my day.' A Leo Sayer song came to mind, 'I'm a one-man band.'

I was very nervous, but felt my game coming together as the match progressed. I caught Gordon Greenidge very early on and Richards charged at one ball, from Geoff Miller, that turned outside the line on the legside. Some critics later described it as 'an easy stumping chance' which annoyed me at first but then made me laugh. For me to have collected that ball I would have needed arms like Joel Garner's. As to batting at Old Trafford, the situation had become faintly ridiculous by the time I reached the crease and I wasn't very sensible in getting out to the shot I played. Perhaps I should have been more selfish, said to myself that England could not win in any circumstances, carried on batting and assembled 40 or 50 that would have looked good in the scorebook.

Another incident from Old Trafford that will stick in the memory was my running out of Malcolm Marshall. Naturally I was delighted, feeling cock-a-hoop when Neil Foster strolled across and said, very quietly, 'I wouldn't be doing that too often if I were you. Malcolm might get offended and he'd be a bad enemy. When Malcolm says it's Friday, it's Friday.'

On Saturday, at Trent Bridge, England won to level the score. My keeping was back to form and the only regret I have about the match is, again, the way I got out near the end of the England innings. The match was won and Ian Botham and I could have taken England home with ones and twos; it wasn't necessary to try slamming fours, yet both Ian and I got ourselves out trying to play grandstand shots, thus creating an unnecessary and artificial crisis.

I hugely enjoyed the scene: a big crowd; complete attention on every ball; Derek Pringle bowling so well and then making a fabulous catch to dismiss Richards. Looking back I wish someone had watered the beer at Trent Bridge.

By early evening the crowd were singing, 'England, England'. Everyone was feeling pretty jubilant and I remember catching Viv's expression: a steely glare. I thought to myself, 'He'll be trying again at Lord's', and he was.

But it was a win to remember. I grabbed a stump as a souvenir for Tommy Morley, landlord of my local, The Scotland, and then set off with Gail for Lord's, full of foreboding at what Viv had in store for England.

It was fairly obvious to all that Lord's would be a seamer's pitch so I was surprised when England went in with four seamers and a spinner. This meant that Geoff Miller would be expected to bowl his full eleven overs which I thought, remembering that the boundaries are so compressed at Lord's on these occasions – the distance between midwicket and cover is less than on many league grounds in Yorkshire – would be a very risky business.

Viv still had that determined, hard look about him and I said to Gail, 'He loves Lord's, he loves the big occasion. He'll try everything not to be outdone here.'

However, there was an even bigger surprise awaiting me. We were loosening up under Bernard Thomas when David Gower came across and spoke to Ian Botham. Replied Ian, 'Well, I can keep wicket standing back.'

My heart sank. I thought they were going to drop me. Then the captain came across and said, 'You are very quickly coming into the reckoning as our sixth bowler.'

'Are you serious?' I asked.

'Very serious' said Gower.

All I could say to that was, 'You know I'll try my best.' Nothing more happened in that direction, although there was a little byplay on the field. I would say something like, 'I fancy this end, skipper.'

He came back, 'Just keep loose.'

Again we had to face Joel Garner off his new, long run, bowling exceptionally quickly and still gaining that nasty, unpredictable bounce. There can never have been a bowler in cricket like him. He's a phenomenon.

Garner was backed up by some astonishing fielding from Roger Harper. The West Indies say he is the best in the world and the catch he took to dismiss Botham in the deep,

54

Above: As the 1984 season progressed, our young players became more and more vital. Here is the 'sixth form' watching play. From left to right: Ashley Metcalfe, Paul Booth, Martyn Moxon, Paul Jarvis, Stuart Fletcher. In the distance 'Mr Chips' (coach Doug Padgett)

Below: Temple of Repose, Cabinet of Secrets. The Yorkshire dressing room at Headingley, tidier than usual, complete with barley water, orange squash, a pot of tea and a pensive captain

The Yorkshire team. Back row, left to right: A. Sidebottom (Arnie), J.D. Love (Lovey), M.D. Moxon (Froggy), S. Oldham (Esso), S.D. Fletcher (Fletch), P.E. Robinson (Red), I.G. Swallow (Chicken). Front row: P. Carrick (Fergie), G.B. Stevenson (Moonbeam), D.L. Bairstow (Bluey), G. Boycott (Boycs), K. Sharp (Sharpy)

Left: Paul Jarvis watching with fascination as I tape up my hands

Opposite: It was much easier doing this sort of thing when I played football for Bradford City

Below: Martyn Moxon gets his county cap and a pat from me on the morning of 26 May, just before the Headingley Roses match. A month later he was selected to play for England

Above: The Headingley Roses match: Yorkshire v Lancashire, 26 May. Lancashire's Alan Ormrod just avoids a run-out

Almighty Arnie: Sidebottom bowls to Ormrod in the Headingley Roses match. Had Arnie sustained form and fitness, Yorkshire might have had a very successful season

Yorkshire's captain in action at the Headingley Roses match

Richard Lumb, 'the well-dressed short leg', must never be caught short of insurance running with his hands virtually on the floor, was certainly world class. If all that wasn't enough, there came yet another virtuoso performance from King Richards, fulfilling all my premonitions about the day. For all that, I wasn't unhappy with my own performances. I felt I had kept wicket better in the three games for England than I had done in the previous weeks for Yorkshire. I could have done better with the bat but I wasn't brought into the side to hang about. I was supposed to get runs quickly and that was what I tried to do.

Did I miss Richards down the legside? It was never a catch, and even if I had got a hand to the ball, umpire David Constant confirmed afterwards that Viv would have been back in his crease.

The atmosphere in the England dressing room, despite losing the first Texaco Trophy, was tremendous. I'm still laughing at a story of Neil Foster's about Derek Randall in Australia. Derek was reading a book when it was his turn to go into bat. He handed the book over to Foster saying, 'The hero's right in the mire. Read on a few pages. Get him out of it', then went off whistling. Pure 'Arkle'.

I heard the bad news at Tunbridge Wells after rejoining Yorkshire for the match against Kent. In the dressing room on the Saturday morning the attendant, whom we know as Rocky, called out to me, 'There's David Gower on the phone for you.' As I went to take the call I could sense the whole of the Yorkshire dressing room was tense.

David thanked me for my help, said he was sorry there wasn't a place in the Test side for me. I replied, 'I understand. Thank you for calling me. You can count on me when you want me.' I could tell he was a little embarrassed. I am older than him, I've had a phone call like that before and it's a very nasty job to tell a player he's not wanted. David Gower also wrote to me, confirming the conversation and I, for one, was impressed with the trouble he'd taken to break unpleasant news.

When I got back to the dressing room the lads could tell from my expression what had happened. The comment I

55

remember came from Arnie Sidebottom, 'Thank God for that. I'm sorry you're not in but I'm glad for us.' Home is where the heart is.

In my absence Yorkshire had lost a day's play and drawn a Britannic Championship match with Sussex at Sheffield and then had gone on to repeat the experience against Somerset at Middlesbrough. But an astonishing 81 off 29 balls, a John Player League record, by Graham Stevenson gave us our first victory as defending champions against Somerset in the Sunday League. And, if I needed reminding, my deputy Steven Rhodes, the Young England wicket-keeper, had been winning glowing notices in my absence with England.

Wednesday, 6 June

Sussex v Yorkshire

at Hove

Yorkshire beat Sussex by 37 runs

I rejoined the team in Hove, where we were to meet Sussex in the Benson & Hedges quarter-final. Important as that match was, it was also vital that Yorkshire improved on their championship performances after having such a good start to the season. I know the Yorkshire public. They are happy to see us succeed in one-day competitions but nothing will convince them that we are a side worthy of the name of Yorkshire until we win the county championship again.

I arrived in Hove before the rest of the team, who had a long and wearing journey down from Middlesbrough. As I reached the hotel I saw a police incident unit opposite, walked across to discover that there had been a murder in the bus shelter the previous night. I rang Graham Stevenson in Middlesbrough to explain how to find the hotel and passed on the news thinking, afterwards, it might not have been a wise thing to do. Some of the team might have regarded it as a far from lucky omen.

For the second time in the summer I lost the toss. John Barclay, the Sussex captain, is an Old Etonian. He threw up a pound coin, I called heads, it came down tails whereupon John proclaimed, in that unique accent, 'Oh, God, I don't know what to do. I think you'd better have a bat.' He caused our lads some amusement later when he called down the wicket to Garth Le Roux, Sussex's giant South African fast bowler, 'Come along, Garth, just one more heroic over.'

Our assessment of the Hove pitch was that it was slower than normal and more suited to our cricket than theirs, Garth being the kind of bowler who bangs in the ball. And so it proved. Boycott and Moxon gave us a splendid start with Boycott playing some unbelievable shots, for him. He whacked Tony Pigott over long on a blow that was a couple of feet short of a six, he ran down the pitch to hit Dermot Reeve over wide long on, he got after John Barclay and Chris Waller. I was delighted because it proved my point that he is perfectly capable of improvising and pushing the score along when he's relaxed and in a confident mood.

I went in higher up the order than I wished, bowing to the arguments of Boycott and Carrick that the time was ripe for me to go in and swing. Boycott kept repeating, 'I'm only giving you advice. I'm not trying to tell you what to do. You've got to make the decisions.' So when I got out, almost immediately, I made this my excuse, which was wrong. I should have trusted my instincts and left the batting order alone.

As it happened Jim Love and Neil Hartley came along to produce another powerful partnership that brought us a total of 261 runs and left us feeling fairly confident. I didn't think our position invulnerable: Sussex are a strong batting side and this was a slow pitch. We needed to bowl and field well to win and that is exactly what we did, so well in fact that we received many messages of congratulations afterwards (the match was televised), the gist being that Yorkshire had produced a high-class professional team performance.

Martyn Moxon provided a good bowling spell. Phil Carrick was upset because I didn't bowl him at all, but accepted my explanation that I didn't think it was the occasion to do so.

What delighted me most about our bowling was the performance of Stuart Fletcher, especially in the closing spell. For a nineteen-year-old to come back and bowl so tightly to so dangerous a player as Le Roux, who is capable of hitting any bowler for miles, was a terrific plus for Yorkshire. The lad is a diamond.

Saturday, 9 June–Tuesday, 12 June

Kent v Yorkshire
at Tunbridge Wells

Kent drew with Yorkshire

Yorkshire moved on to Kent at Tunbridge Wells in good heart after a pleasant day's golf in Worthing. I won the toss again, decided to bat, told the team I wanted as many runs as possible on the first day, but there was a slight middle-order collapse and overall it wasn't one of Yorkshire's better batting performances. Had we batted better on that first day we would have left ourselves more time on the Tuesday and probably have won the game.

Martyn Moxon played yet another fine innings, adding fuel to the rumours that he would be in the England Test side at Lord's. My old team-mate Philip Sharpe, now an England selector, was present and I made my views known to him very forcibly. I have no fears for Martyn's future. But I do not want him to go through what might be a very demoralizing experience in his first full season in first-class cricket.

We may have failed to clinch victory on the last afternoon because we began too well! Kent were 18-4 at tea and nothing to play for but a draw. Had they been 90-4 they might have kept going and given us a chance to bowl them out. Arnie Sidebottom bowled well again, especially in the first innings when a couple of snicks went begging. I moved Boycott out of slips and replaced him with Moxon, who immediately began taking catches and cheered up Arnie.

I left Kent with my admiration for Alan Knott undiminished. He's been called a showman, he has a few little mannerisms but he remains a magnificent craftsman behind the stumps. He's changed his stance over the years – he now places his hands outside his feet and he doesn't go down as far, to ease the strain on the groin – but he remains a superb example to us all. Whenever I see Knotty I'm always conscious of watching one of the greatest ever wicket-keepers.

Kent v Yorkshire
at Canterbury

Yorkshire beat Kent by 6 wickets

Our Sunday win at Canterbury, after a delightful drive through the hop country of Kent, was achieved by what was then a very confident Yorkshire side. But, as now almost by habit, we caused a minor controversy.

I couldn't fail to win the toss, sent in Kent and Old Reliable, Steve Oldham, bowled like a dream and pegged them down. I was standing up to Oldham when I caught the Kent captain, Chris Tavaré – the ball disappearing between my legs. I yelled an appeal. Everyone looked baffled. Where was the ball? 'I've caught it, I've caught it' I shouted, but with my gloves on I couldn't produce it from between my thighs. Everybody was laughing except Tavaré, who had been struggling so hard to rediscover the form that had made him an England regular.

Kent have always been a difficult side to beat in one-day matches, especially at Canterbury. We had to score 165 to win and recognized it would not be easy with 'Deadly' Derek Underwood still seeking his 300th wicket in the John Player League and standing on 299.

We began well; Martyn Moxon playing superbly well, hitting one huge straight six off Underwood. Then we lost a couple of wickets and I went in to bat with Underwood and the Australian Test bowler Terry Alderman still with overs left to bowl. As I walked out I looked back towards the pavilion and saw a huge thundercloud gathering in the distance. I signalled for Graham Stevenson to pad up to follow me in, realizing that to win we might have to make our last runs in a very great hurry if we were to beat the weather. Fortunately we were already ahead on the scoring rate.

It was at this point that we ran into what I have to regard as a lack of flexibility in the rules of the Player League competition. During the Kent innings Chris Cowdrey had pulled a muscle. A good deal of time was taken up in organizing a runner, which cost something like five to ten minutes. This not only cut into their batting time but also, of course, reduced ours, as we would be allowed only the same number of overs as Kent. Originally the umpires said that they would allow the time lost to be made up but then, when Kent lost a couple of wickets in their 38th over, the umpires ruled again and said that would be the innings limit. Kent had calculated on batting 40 overs and so had we. Suddenly both sides had lost 12 balls, which may not seem a lot but can be crucial in a 40-over match. There ought to be a provision made for time lost through injuries.

Hampshire v Yorkshire

at Basingstoke

Hampshire drew with Yorkshire

Our southern tour continued with a championship match against Hampshire at Basingstoke. I was very disappointed over our failure to beat Kent and anxious to make up those lost points against a team who were without their two great West Indians, Malcolm Marshall and Gordon Greenidge. I couldn't help feeling envious of captains like Hampshire's Nick Pocock who can, when West Indies are not touring, call on two such power-houses whenever the team looks like running into trouble.

Stuart Fletcher had strained a tendon in Kent. It was nothing serious, but with a Benson & Hedges semi-final due to be played the following week I thought it best to give him a few days' rest. As a youngster in his first season he had taken on a great deal of responsibility.

What I wasn't to know was that in resting Fletcher I set off a chain reaction. Great-hearted Arnie Sidebottom just about bowled himself into the ground over three very hot days at Basingstoke and then had to miss the next championship match, against Derbyshire at Harrogate. Had both Stuart and Arnie been fully fit for both fixtures we might well have won them. Simon Dennis was still recovering from his twisted ankle and neither of my two senior bowlers, Carrick and Stevenson, were in form.

I won the toss again, the *Daily Telegraph* giving the dressing room a laugh the following morning by commenting that I won the toss so often I should 'holiday in Las Vegas'. The sky was overcast and the pitch hard, so I reasoned that the ball might move and then turn quickly later. Chris Smith was having a spell of terrible luck but Paul Terry applied himself well. Arnie bowled like a Trojan reminding me again that but for the ban following his brief South African trip he would surely be an England player.

I had no complaints about our batting. Moxon dragged a ball on to his stumps. He doesn't play the pull shot too well. He tends to crouch when, with his height, he might be far better off standing upright and driving the ball wide of mid on.

For the second match in succession Ian Swallow did the night-watchman's job and did it well. He's small, looks much younger than his twenty-two years, but he shows a great deal of talent and application. He's a gutsy little player and the fact that I intend to leave him out of the team very shortly is no reflection on the advance he has made since he was first selected. I didn't want to overstretch him in his first season and it is asking too much of any lad to come into the first team straight away and bowl as well as his predecessor, Ray Illingworth.

Yorkshire reached 401 without anyone getting a century, another good team effort, and we shall not hear the last of Steve Oldham's hooking of Elvis Reifer, for four, for a very long time. Having then removed three of their leading batsmen by the end of the second day, our next victory the following morning seemed only a matter of time.

Alas for all our hopes. I intended to use seam at one end, where the bounce was unpredictable, and spin at the other where there was turn. Sadly, Phil Carrick had a very poor day, bowling far too many full deliveries that caused the batsmen few problems, and Hampshire were able to block out hour after hour. Had Carrick bowled well the match would have been over by three o'clock.

In the end we became involved in a mad run chase, 85 needed to win off 12 overs. Having put some of the blame for the draw on Carrick, I should also add that the match, even at the point when we batted again, was still very winnable. A regular momentum of scoring is vital in an innings as brief as that and we slipped up when we lost two wickets very quickly, Kevin Sharp having a mow and Carrick dragging on. We thought of sending in Boycott at four or five but I decided against it. He's basically a touch player and what we needed, on a ground with small boundaries and with every ball vital, was brute force.

Having conducted the inquest on our own performance I should add that Mark Nicholas played exceptionally well for his century, a highly responsible, capable innings that saved the game for his team and a performance of which any captain would be very proud.

Saturday, 16 June–Tuesday, 19 June

Yorkshire v Derbyshire

at Harrogate

Yorkshire drew with Derbyshire

Despite our failure to win championship matches at Tunbridge Wells and Basingstoke, we returned home to Harrogate to play Derbyshire in pretty good spirits. I knew that we would be without Arnie Sidebottom, who was again plagued with sore shins. But I had a shock when I saw the Harrogate pitch: because of the drought in the North it was bare and dry, looking something like the bed of a dried-up reservoir. I realized that I would have to play two spinners and leave out a seam bowler. Jim Love looked in to see how the lads were and found himself in the team; otherwise Metcalfe would have come into the side.

I lost the toss and soon came to the conclusion that, once you had played yourself in on that pitch, there wasn't a great deal the bowlers could do to get you out. The ball bounced less than knee high, it never seamed, it never swung.

John Morris, Derbyshire's young batsman from Crewe, scored a fine 100 and is clearly an outstanding prospect, well balanced with shots all round the wicket. If that weren't enough, Derbyshire had one of the world's best opening batsmen, John Wright of New Zealand, coming in at number five and, as might be expected, adding another century; nearly two in fact, finishing with 176.

I was very surprised to find Derbyshire continuing to bat on the Monday morning – the two sides had been through the Chesterfield fracas on the Sunday – and batting slowly, too. Eventually we had to get to win on the final day, and the match trailed off into a disappointing draw when we were obliged to give up the chase. I couldn't throw the responsibility of winning or losing a match on youngsters like Stuart Fletcher and Ian Swallow in their first full season, and Neil Hartley had a broken toe.

I shall chiefly remember the match for the fact that I had to declare when, if I had batted on, Philip Robinson might have followed Ashley Metcalfe and Martyn Moxon to the distinction of having scored a century on debut. I've nothing but admiration for the lad's attitude. The first time he came into the dressing room, someone said to him half-jokingly, 'Where do you bat then, Robbo?'

He just smiled and said, 'Onywheer tha' wants.'

When he came into the dressing room at Harrogate, not out on 74, I said immediately, 'I'm sorry, Robbo, but I had to declare.' He just shrugged and replied, 'That's all right. It'll do for starters.'

Philip shows a refreshing attitude towards the game: he's very open to advice and instruction; he listens to everything he's told and then adapts the advice to the game as he sees it; he has great powers of concentration and doesn't seem to have any nerves at all. His approach is superb.

The composition of the batting order was beginning to prove a problem and, in the light of what happened later, my attempts to sort things out now seem a little odd. The fact is – and I remember David Gower being quoted on this very point – that no captain can ever afford to look too far ahead. He has to make his decisions on the conditions applying at the time of that match, or that innings, or of that bowling change.

I had been on the verge of leaving Richard Lumb out of the championship side. As he is an old friend of mine, I didn't relish the prospect of having to break the news to him. But before that could happen he had to withdraw through a minor injury and, like it or not, the impression was growing that Geoff Boycott's regular partner for the past eleven years was fading out of the side.

I had said to the dressing room, before the season started, that I knew occasions would arise when regular players would have to be dropped. It may have seemed like an apology in advance. No one likes to upset old friends and I know the older members of the side would soon sense my embarrassment when the time came.

So I was very grateful to Jim Love who had come up to me before Harrogate and said, 'I know I'm not playing well, Stanley. If you feel you need to leave me out, I'll understand.' And when it was necessary to leave Jim out, very shortly afterwards, I didn't have to say anything to him. A capped player still has a traditional prestige and dignity in the Yorkshire dressing room, dating from the days, under Hawke and Sellers, when it was easier to win an England cap than Yorkshire's. A capped player is supposed to be established for the next ten years or more – a man with a definite place in the side and a definite job to do – and isn't left out lightly.

Derbyshire v Yorkshire
at Chesterfield

Yorkshire beat Derbyshire by 44 runs

This proved a match that will be remembered for some very distasteful episodes, but it also had its compensations in the batting performances from two twenty-year-old Yorkshiremen. Now that Yorkshire had registered Philip Robinson from Keighley, it was an ideal opportunity to give him his first taste of senior cricket. Jim Love was still worried by his viral infection, so I rang Ashley Metcalfe who had made such an impression with his century in his first team debut, against Notts at Bradford in 1983.

Philip, a chunky man with a very cool temperament who looks older than his age, was immediately dubbed 'Red Robbo'. He won this praise from Phil Carrick after our victory, 'Looking at Robbo, he seems as if he has never been out of the side.' Ashley, too, was clearly ready for senior cricket, a point he was to make even more forcibly later on. Both scored 39 with innings of very contrasting styles and our total of 225-6 gave Derbyshire a difficult task, especially when they were finally committed to scoring 91 off the last 10 overs. Phil Carrick again did a valiant job in restraining their middle order batsmen and taking 3 wickets.

The difficult situation that arose after the game resulted

67

directly from the all-afternoon drinking. Since then the Derbyshire and Chesterfield clubs have put some restrictions on Sunday licensing hours but this followed a nasty scene.

During the match there had been a great deal of banter from Derbyshire supporters, stemming from the fact that I had played for England in the Texaco Trophy matches and that Derbyshire's great wicket-keeper, Bob Taylor, had been left out. I expected that, laughed at some of the cracks, and got on with the game.

As I was walking off after our victory, I reached the steps going up to the pavilion and heard a man say over my shoulder, 'Bairstow, you'll never be as f———g good as Bobby Taylor. You're a f———g wanker.' He then kicked me in the back of the leg.

I turned round, saying, 'Don't kick me', and pushed him. As he was so drunk, he fell over backwards. But as I turned again to go back up the steps, he climbed up and again kicked me in the leg. A Yorkshire player, following me, then knocked him down and said, 'Don't you kick anyone in the back.'

As the rest of the team filed up the steps, they had beer thrown over them. A drunken mob gathered outside the dressing room, shouting insults, and it wasn't until the police arrived and arrested a few for being drunk and disorderly that they dispersed.

Yorkshire rightly ordered an enquiry the following morning after the story had appeared in several newspapers. The player who had knocked down the drunk came forward and said he felt perfectly justified in defending another member of the team who was being attacked from behind. Yorkshire also took a statement from me and after discussions with Derbyshire declared the matter ended.

But they couldn't end the cause of the trouble. This kind of ugly scene has been coming for a long time as more and more of what you could call all-day drinkers realize that a county cricket club on a Sunday afternoon gives them a perfect excuse. What happened to us could easily happen to another team elsewhere, with much more serious consequences.

When drink's in, wit's out.

Yorkshire v Warwickshire
at Headingley

Yorkshire lost by 3 runs

As the Benson & Hedges semi-final drew near, we were all nervous. We hadn't expected to get this far in the competition but, as I kept pointing out, we were there on merit. We had a well-balanced side and we had only marginally failed to beat Warwickshire when set to score 260 in the zonal match at Edgbaston.

Now we were at home at Headingley, we had enormous support from a packed ground, and I felt my job was to get the team to see the match as it was; another 55-over game in which we had every reason to feel that we were as good as any side in the country.

Having made that point to them, I had to admit that we had suffered a heavy blow at Harrogate. When Neil Hartley was hit on the right toe by Paul Newman, the first prediction was that he could be out of the team for three to six weeks after examinations had shown three breaks in the bone. In fact, Neil being Neil, he was back much quicker than that, wearing a plastic cover over the toe.

But he was missing from our semi-final team and his

69

absence, more than any other factor, turned the match against us. Neil was a three-in-one player in limited-overs matches; my stand-in bowler, stand-in batsman and expert boundary fielder – fast, accurate with a superb throwing arm. Yorkshire did not have the resources to make up such a loss.

However, that morning I refused to worry over our deficiencies. I concentrated on our strengths, repeating over and over to myself that, given a target, we could chase anything, almost, and still win. And we nearly did just that.

The Bairstow luck held; I won the toss and sent in Warwickshire. Everything went as usual. Arnie had some abominable luck again, making the batsmen play and miss without taking the wickets. He had had a conversation with Bob Appleyard at Harrogate, and Bob had asked him, 'Why do you beat the bat by six inches?'

Replied Arnie, with due respect to a man who had bowled for England, who once took 200 wickets in a season and who had recently been appointed an additional bowling coach, 'I don't know. I just grip the seam, run up and bowl.'

Bob added, 'You should be able to control the amount of seam or swing. Three inches is much more difficult for the batsman to judge than six inches.' Arnie was baffled.

I caught David Smith early on, but our troubles then began at Graham Stevenson's end. I backed Stevo; I wanted him in the side because I believe that he is an England all-rounder who should have been alongside Ian Botham in the Test side for the last five years. The problem is that the last man in England to believe or to accept that assessment of his ability is Graham Stevenson.

This was one of Stevo's rock-bottom days. His 11 overs cost Yorkshire 70 runs, a tragedy. Add the 19 extras and it will be clear to anyone that Warwickshire were given a fair number of the 276 runs they eventually assembled. Bowling wides and no-balls had become a major handicap to Yorkshire in all the one-day competitions; some Sundays we were, in effect, presenting our opponents with as many as two extra overs.

Not that Warwickshire's big total dismayed us. The resolve was still there. We would have been much happier chasing 250, obviously, but there was no gloom in the dressing room. The feeling was that Yorkshire could win the match, as, of course, we should have done.

Geoff Boycott was out to Chris Old, opening the face of his bat and trying to run one, something that kept happening to him around this time. Martyn Moxon played some dazzling shots to reach 50 off 81 balls, at which point two so-called supporters ran on to congratulate him. I don't know whether this upset his concentration – it can't have helped – but he was out sweeping soon afterwards.

I was amazed when Peter Parfitt gave me the Gold Award as Man of the Match. It should have gone to either Alvin Kallicharran of Warwickshire or to Kevin Sharp. Kevin played superbly until he was out to a silly shot; he should never get bowled trying to cut. Young Philip Robinson was probably a little overawed but the match was still very winnable when Stevo and I came together. We added 71 in 10 overs, had a little luck with misfields, but were finally beaten by what looked like an intervention from Fate.

I was out to a dazzling boundary catch by a man who had just been moved five yards. A yard either side of him would have given me a six. When Graham was out the field had just been moved again. He hit high, attempting to clear the field, but the man who had moved was Bob Willis, one of the tallest players in the game. No other man in the Warwickshire side could have reached that catch.

To lose by three runs flattened the dressing room for the first time. A defeat by 50 or 60 runs would have been bearable because we could then accept we had been outplayed. To lose by three, when chasing 276, was tragic. Derek Hodgson rang me the following day and cheered me a little by pointing out that the team had made friends and won prestige, even in defeat. True, but as I've said before, who remembers beaten semi-finalists?

I was so low that when I got home, Gail asked me what I would have done had Yorkshire won. I said we would have had a party. 'Right,' said Gail. 'Ring up the team. We'll have a barbecue.' And we did, with as many of the team, with wives and girlfriends attending, as possible.

Derek Hodgson had given me a bottle of Moet et Chandon after our championship win at Taunton. 'Don't drink it now,' he advised. 'Wait until a rainy day.' Gail and I opened it to toast a sunnier time.

Saturday, 23 June–Tuesday, 26 June

Northamptonshire v Yorkshire

at Northampton

Yorkshire beat Northamptonshire by an innings and 34 runs

Our Benson & Hedges gloom did not last for long. We arrived in Northampton to find a pitch worthy of considerable study. It was covered in patches of green tufty grass, interspersed with cracks. It was obvious it would break up rapidly and was immediately dubbed 'The Burma Road'. I had no doubt it would be win the toss, win the match.

I duly won the toss. Boycott got himself out once again opening the face before Martyn Moxon and Ashley Metcalfe raised a century stand. What we didn't know is that during that innings Martyn was hit in the ribs by a ball from the South African fast bowler Rupert Hanley and that, after an examination on the following Monday, he was withdrawn from the England team because of a suspected

72

fractured rib. Not that Martyn got much sympathy from the dressing room. 'Froggy's that soft, a ball from David Steele could crack his ribs' was one joke.

Martyn should really have had the century he deserved. We lost some time to poor light that Saturday evening but then, thanks to Arnie and young Paul Booth, we forced a follow-on. Eighteen-year-old Paul, a slow left bowler from Huddersfield, took 3-21 in 22 overs, perhaps an auspicious performance. Phil Carrick, our senior left-arm spinner, was suffering from a heavy cold, but there's no doubt in my mind that when he saw that there was a youngster proving he was capable of taking his place in the team he was spurred into some kind of action.

Even then, Fergie was lucky to return his best bowling analysis of the season. I'd given Paul the last over of Monday evening from the Football Stand End which meant, inevitably, that Carrick bowled the first over on Tuesday from the Pavilion End. The result was that Fergie produced one of the finest bowling spells of his entire career, 6-32, giving us a victory by an innings and 34, the biggest Yorkshire championship win for four years. Had he bowled like that at Tunbridge Wells and Basingstoke, Yorkshire would have been close to the top of the championship table.

Northamptonshire's faith in their powers of survival on the Northampton pitch was summed up by Rupert Hanley, their number 10 batsman, who, on the Tuesday morning, had told his babysitter he would be home for lunch. It was on the Tuesday morning, too, that Martyn had to ring the chairman of selectors to warn him about the rib injury. He hadn't felt more than a little discomfort until making a fine diving slip catch on the Monday.

I was sorry that Martyn should miss his chance of playing at Lord's against West Indies, but I also have to admit to a certain amount of relief. I explained to the *Daily Telegraph*, 'I happen to think that Martyn is the best young opening batsman in England. He has every chance of becoming one of the great names in the game.

'I am not afraid that he will fail. But I think the selectors are risking giving him a demoralising experience in what is after all his first full season.'

Northamptonshire v Yorkshire

at Luton

Yorkshire beat Northamptonshire by 4 wickets

We left Northampton for Luton and the Sunday John Player League match in convoy, listening to every news bulletin for confirmation of Martyn Moxon's selection for England. None of us knew, of course, that Martyn was already carrying a cracked rib.

Yorkshire were knocking up in practice on the Luton ground when the selection was announced, putting us all in good spirits for what we expected to be a very hard match. Luton is renowned as a high-scoring ground; Wayne Larkins had hit 172 not out against Warwickshire on that pitch in 1983, and when Northants got away to a good start I was beginning to fear a repetition. I had to switch my bowlers around, hoping to find a combination that would contain Northants who, given the opportunity, are capable of shredding any attack.

Eventually Phil Carrick proved to be the man to tie them down, bowling a very good spell. But it was Geoff Boycott who best summed up the situation. He strolled across the pitch to say, 'Northants are looking at this as a 260–275 pitch. It's not. It's a 200 pitch.'

He was right. There was a little life in it, the odd ball was seaming, enough to encourage Stuart Fletcher to return for an excellent closing spell. When we batted, Yorkshire were cruising to victory, though a couple of contentious umpiring decisions upset the order and it needed Arnie, ever reliable even if the lads do believe he's made of sugar, to crack a couple of fours and make sure we got home comfortably.

For the second Sunday in succession there was a lot of rowdiness around the public bars and the police had to be called. Once again, I think I have to make the point that unless the cricket authorities do take some action on this issue there will be very serious trouble somewhere.

But overall Yorkshire had a good weekend and we were in good spirits. Allan Lamb's concern about his England place was reflected in his comment when he heard the team: 'Oh, they've kept me in, have they?' Curiously, that day was a turning point in Allan's career, because he went off to hit two fine centuries against the West Indies. Yorkshire, meanwhile, had no inkling of the storms that were about to break.

Notts v Yorkshire
at Trent Bridge

Notts drew with Yorkshire

We had had an exhilarating victory over Notts at Headingley and, although Clive Rice and his men had gained a minor revenge with a Sunday victory in Hull, we knew that Notts, keen and strong enough to regain the championship, would be waiting for us at Trent Bridge. Naturally there was a great deal of discussion and speculation in the Yorkshire party as to what kind of surface Notts would have prepared for us. Too many of our players were expecting demons before they actually got out on the grass.

In fact, the pitch had been placed on the right-hand side of the square which, we were told, was the part that bounced! When I walked out on the square Clive Rice and Richard Hadlee were already there. I said casually, looking at a rich expanse of green, 'I'm glad the white lines have been painted in, otherwise I wouldn't have known where we were playing.'

Hadlee grinned and replied, 'You didn't expect anything else, did you?'

The irony of it all was that at the end of the game the Notts head groundsman, Ron Allsopp, thanked me for speaking to him. He explained, 'I'm not getting much from our lads. They reckon it wasn't quick or bouncy enough.'

But I wasn't to know that when I won the toss. The pitch looked both damp and green and it was with some glee that I told Clive Rice we would field. The result was that the pitch did virtually nothing to help our bowlers. Tim Robinson assembled yet another big 100, to be followed by the ominous presence of Derek Randall, who again tormented us. He was on 99 when I heard him call down the pitch to his partner, 'Back up, I haven't got one yet this year.' The 100 delighted the sparse crowd, but there wasn't too much joy in our dressing room because it had become all too clear that we were running out of bowling resources.

Stuart Fletcher, the bowling find of the season, had to drop out with a recurring pelvic strain. Arnie bowled on the first day but it was obvious that his shins needed resting again.

Graham Stevenson dropped out with heel trouble. Paul Booth, after bowling so well at Northampton, had gone home because we knew we would not be playing two spinners at Trent Bridge. In effect, I was left with only two fit and experienced bowlers, Phil Carrick and Steve Oldham. Steve was magnificent and his new dressing-room nickname of 'Grandad' was bestowed with a great deal of respect and affection. To make up the numbers, we had to send for Paul Jarvis, who was struggling to find his form in the second team, and Simon Dennis, who was still recovering from his Roses match injury.

Having made all the excuses, I have to add that Notts batted very well and deserved their runs. Clive Rice declared after 100 overs and Yorkshire lost two wickets that night: Ashley Metcalfe was caught miraculously by Randall at slip; and then Paul Jarvis, who had volunteered for the night-watchman's job, was out third ball. Kevin Sharp, who had said in the dressing room, 'I'll be in tonight', was proved right even quicker than he expected.

The collapse continued the following morning and Yorkshire were 80-5 when I arrived at the wicket to play, in

77

my own opinion, my best innings of the season up to that date. The pitch had become slightly quicker, which helped, but it also helped Hadlee, who is certainly one of the best, if not the best opening bowler in the world.

When I left, caught at slip, it seemed there might be another Yorkshire collapse. But Yorkshire scrambled a third batting bonus point, Simon Dennis pulling Eddie Hemmings for two sixes into the Hound Road Stand. The unlikely partnership of Dennis and Oldham eventually took us to a fourth batting point and when the pair returned to the dressing room, Steve was greeted with a barrage of applause and calls of 'Well done, Wally [Hammond].'

We then had to listen while 'Grandad' explained that the bat had felt like an extension of his left arm, how the ball had come off nothing but the middle of that bat, how each and every one of his strokes was planned and executed.

All this went down very well until, in the course of discussion about the bowling, Boycott declared of Oldham, 'I can bowl as fast as he can.' He received a withering glance from Steve and this retort, 'Maybe *you* can but *I've* had to do your batting today.' Anyone who has seen Boycott and Oldham bat on the same day will appreciate the humour of that remark.

The dressing room, having previously decided that Arnie Sidebottom was made of sugar, then addressed the same label to Notts' very popular Kenyan-born batsman, Basharat Hassan. 'Basher' was hit in the chest by a bouncer from Simon Dennis and turned to me, rubbing the spot, to say, 'Bluey, that hurt.' A fatal thing to admit, of course, for Simon was then encouraged to give him another bouncer.

'Let it go, Simon,' someone shouted. 'He's made of sugar.'

Even 'Basher' broke out laughing when Phil Carrick added, 'Aye, Demerara.'

Sadly, a hard match but a good-natured match with a lot of laughs was only the prelude to a disaster.

Saturday, 30 June–Tuesday, 3 July

Yorkshire v Essex
at Headingley

Essex beat Yorkshire by an innings and 153 runs

Yorkshire were unbeaten in the Britannic Championship until this match. When we did lose, we did it in style, suffering our heaviest defeat at Headingley since the ground opened in 1891, and the seventh worst defeat in the county's history. You could say that all the chickens had come home to roost.

For various reasons, mostly to do with injuries, the team was shorn of Moxon, Lumb, Stevenson, Sidebottom and Fletcher. I was horrified to discover that the pitch was green, something I didn't expect to find in the prevailing dry weather, and something that played right into Essex's hands, with their strength in seam bowling.

Had Yorkshire had a full seam attack I wouldn't have hesitated about sending Essex in to bat, but in the circumstances I felt I had to take advantage of the toss and Yorkshire paid the consequences. We needed a brown dry pitch that would turn later if we were to match the champions; instead Essex were presented with conditions they couldn't have bettered in Chelmsford.

As I say, we had to bat and we did it disastrously, playing without application and, it seemed, purpose. Essex, on the other hand, had John Lever, who bowled 25 overs that day with a bandage round his stomach to cover a weeping abscess. How much pain or discomfort he suffered we don't know; we do know how much application and courage he showed. He was a tremendous example to any young fast bowler who wants to succeed, the message being you cannot do it without heart.

Back in the dressing room I told the team, 'It's not over yet. We've got to dig in. Bowl the line, bowl the length. Make them graft for every run.' Sadly, we couldn't even do that.

Had it not been for Steve Oldham, who managed at 34 to bowl 16 successive overs for the Kirkstall Lane End, there would have been an even greater massacre. It was our extra misfortune to come up against Graham Gooch at peak form. He shipped us around for 130, showing again that he's more than England class, he's probably world class, and reminding us how much the ban imposed on those who toured South Africa is costing England. According to the Essex lads, Graham is playing better than ever and he certainly looked to be in that innings.

The only salvation for Yorkshire that day came from Paul Booth, who dismissed Gooch and David East with successive deliveries. It was a cheering little interlude at the end of a long hard day and proved to be only the lull before another storm hit us on the Monday morning.

First, there was a personal crisis of sorts. I had been struggling with a strained Achilles tendon, which was being strapped up every day, and had taken a nasty crack across the knuckles, but these are wear and tear injuries you expect in any season and I was living with them. But that Monday morning I awoke with a terrible rash all over my legs and the lower part of my body.

Worried, I called in to see my doctor near the Headingley ground. His first words to me, before examination, were, 'You look tired out, David. Can you take a week off?' All I could reply was, 'There's no chance of that at present.' He prescribed some cream and tablets and I went on to the ground where Ted Lester, always a source of good advice, told me to rest for the remainder of the match. Keith Fletcher kindly consented to Steven Rhodes' taking over from me as wicket-keeper. I lay down in the dressing room and then watched play for a while. Essex meanwhile marched on to their highest-ever score against Yorkshire, 547, which meant that my team was entering the record book for the wrong reasons, and I didn't like it.

Once Keith Fletcher had declared, we were soon in trouble again and briefly it seemed that I might have had to bat, bad as I felt, on the Monday. Once that danger had passed I went off home and straight to bed, where I slept for about ten hours and woke up feeling considerably better.

I had a net at the ground and decided I was fit enough to play again and bat when necessary. My depression soon returned after what took place in our second innings. Yorkshire were dismissed for 188, Nobby Phillips taking 4 for 28, the last 6 wickets going down for 37. For the first time in the season the situation seemed out of control or, as the dressing room puts it, the wheels came off. When I got back to the dressing room there was a lot of plain talking to be done.

I told everybody that the Yorkshire County Cricket Club, the members and the Yorkshire public simply wouldn't tolerate cricket of that standard. No one, I told them, had a divine right to play in the first team, including myself. I assured them that a contract and a first team cap didn't mean security for a playing career. I reminded them that they had to work at their game every day of their life, that they owed that duty to themselves and the other members of the team. I asked them if they had seen a recent television programme about Birkenhead called 'On the Scrapheap', a documentary on unemployment. I told them, 'It's a very short jump from being where we are to being on the scrapheap, on the dole.' I finished up by saying that if they wanted to play cricket professionally, 'and it's a bloody good living, then you've got to play up to professional standards. You've got to compete and you've got to win.'

81

In my opinion Yorkshire had not been a professional cricket team for a week.

The silence was deafening. I asked Ted, as the senior man present, if he wanted to add anything. He shook his head. I asked Geoff Boycott if he wanted to make any points. He shook his head. I threw it open to anyone. Still silence.

I felt I had said and done the right thing. What I didn't know was that waiting for us down the M6 was an even greater shock.

Sunday, 1 July

Yorkshire v Essex

at Headingley

Essex beat Yorkshire by 17 runs

The Test and County Cricket Board, the game's ruling body in England, has said that counties must not prepare pitches to suit themselves, which is fair and reasonable. Human nature being what it is, any county captain will be keen to find out what kind of surface his team will be expected to play upon, and no captain I know has ever been able to restrain himself from dropping a hint to the groundsman on his likes and dislikes.

Knowing Essex's strength in seamers I'd said to Keith Boyce, the Test groundsman at Leeds, that it would be nice to play on a true flat pitch for the four days against Essex; three in the Britannic Championship, one in the John Player League. On the Saturday morning, I asked Keith what kind of a pitch it would be, and he replied, 'It will be slow and low.' It turned out to be completely the opposite. It was green, quick, it bounced and it went through. Essex couldn't have asked for more help for John Lever and Nobby Phillip if they had prepared it themselves.

I won the toss, again, and said to Keith Fletcher, 'You bat, we'll field.'

He replied, 'Good. I would have batted.'

On the Saturday I had told him, 'We'll bat.'

He then said, 'That's all right. We would have fielded.'

It's one of Fletcher's traits to tell the opposing captain what he would have done had he won the toss.

Arnie Sidebottom was only half-fit but Stuart Fletcher returned to increase our bowling strength. As we also had available Graham Stevenson and Steve Oldham, the attack looked good on paper. While the Essex total of 206 was formidable, it wasn't invulnerable.

Then came Lever. With successive deliveries he dismissed Boycott and Sharp, both caught behind, to become the first bowler to reach 300 wickets in the John Player League. It was a blow that Yorkshire never quite recovered from, although Ashley Metcalfe won a standing ovation from the 8,000 crowd with a sparkling 71 off 91 balls.

A factor overlooked in the Essex victory was Graham Gooch's bowling contribution. He bowled their last five overs and it was amazing to see how a specialist batsman who bowls occasionally could produce so many good yorkers. If he can do it, why can't our specialist bowlers do it? When what is known as 'the thrash' is on – the chase for runs in the remaining overs of a one-day match – the yorker, a ball pitched at the base of the bat, right in the block-hole, is an invaluable delivery; it cannot be pulled, hooked or cut and if the batsman attempts to drive he is bowled. No bowler can deliver six yorkers an over but it shouldn't be beyond our professionals to find three or four in an over.

It was in this match that I realized I was in the middle of

having the worst Sunday League season I've ever had with the bat. When I went to play for England in the Texaco Trophy I had felt in good form, and I think I was probably seeing the ball better, and timing it, than almost anyone in the Yorkshire side. After those matches for England I have felt form drifting away – only one first-class 50 – and no matter what I do I can't seem to get it back. I notice that I've only 450 first-class runs.

Another memory of this weekend of disasters against Essex, and something that was to assume greater significance within days, was the barracking of Essex's West Indian all-rounder, Nobby Phillip. The voice came from somewhere under the poplar trees and angered Nobby sufficiently to make him bowl with a great deal of hostility, so much so that Essex, with their sense of humour, were quick to exploit it.

I was sitting on the balcony with the Essex 12th man, Keith Pont, when I noticed Graham Gooch, at slip, signalling to Pont.

'What does he want?' I asked.

Pont laughed, 'He's wanting me to go round and gee up the crowd into having a go at Nobby to stoke him up.'

We all thought it a good joke until a week later, at Scarborough.

Shropshire v Yorkshire
at Telford

Shropshire beat Yorkshire by 37 runs

I told David Warner afterwards, 'We've been beaten by a team of amateurs, which doesn't say much for our professionals.' This was the third time I had played in a Yorkshire side beaten by 'amateurs' (the previous defeats were by Durham in 1973 and Combined Universities in 1976) and I pray it is the last time.

Again, we had fitness problems. Arnie was still unfit, Graham Stevenson wasn't one hundred per cent, but simply had to play as our senior bowler. As it was a 60-over match there was no question that I had to play five bowlers because, although Martyn Moxon and Neil Hartley, my normal reserve bowlers, were back in the team, both were still convalescing: Martyn was wearing a chest pad to protect his cracked rib and Neil had to wear the plastic cover over his cracked toe. To play five bowlers meant leaving out a batsman and Jim Love took the decision well.

All these risks seemed acceptable before the game. Shropshire had two former first-class players, Mushtaq Mohammed of Pakistan and Northants and Malcolm Nash of Glamorgan, a good enough bowler in his day to be thought unlucky not to have played for England.

Otherwise we were playing against, with the greatest respect, club and weekend cricketers. All we had to do, I believed, was bowl straight and we would win. I won the toss and sent Shropshire in to bat.

I positioned Martyn at first slip and Stevo at second. As I went down to collect the first ball from Steve Oldham I tore my flannels. Martyn said quietly, 'I hope that's not an omen.'

I caught their captain, Johnson, in Oldham's second over and for a while things went well. Then a left-hander, Jones, arrived and Simon Dennis twice got an edge on his bat and both chances, in successive overs, were put down at second slip. Simon removed the other opener but Mushtaq then arrived at the crease. We were all convinced we had him out lbw before he had scored, but that is no reflection on the fine innings he played afterwards. 'Mushy' got away and played well. Once again we bowled too many wides and no-balls, giving them 20 to 30 runs. So Mushtaq was away, we let the left-hander settle in, and we gave runs away. A break at either end would have meant new batsmen coming in, nervous, while our seamers were fresh.

Not that I still had any serious misgivings about scoring 230 to win. Our innings began like a house on fire: Martyn had hit four boundaries on the leg side in next to no time. But then our troubles began again when he departed, to a rather lucky catch by Mushtaq, who pushed the ball up and then managed to hang on to the catch as it fell. After that Yorkshire disintegrated. It's true we had some bad luck, but the overall performance can only be described as bad cricket. Geoff Boycott was singled out for slow scoring, 27 off 25 overs, but he takes no blame from me. Nash began with 12 skilful overs for 15 runs and it was Geoff's job to negotiate that before the later batsmen stepped up the scoring rate. At one point Geoff sent a message, asking me what I wanted him to do. I sent back, 'Stay there and get 100.' In other words, stick at it.

Geoff was out unluckily to a ball that 'stopped', providing a good return catch and it was the middle order,

I'm not laughing: I'm in pain

The fittest team in the world? The West Indies team limbers up before the Texaco Trophy on 31 May

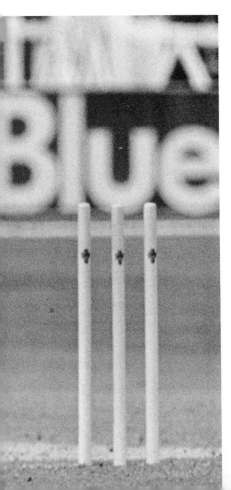

The Texaco Trophy: England v
West Indies, 31 May. The one
occasion when I disagreed with
the umpire's verdict. An
enthusiastic England wicket-
keeper gets the bails off and
believes that he has achieved a
run-out and tells the umpire so.
But the batsman survives

The Texaco Trophy: Garner v Bairstow. (Below) 'Take that, Joel!' (Above) 'Take that, Bluey!'

Above: 'I've heard all your arguments but you can't play 15 men and that's final.' Captains David Gower and Clive Lloyd in debate with umpires, Don Oslear and Dickie Bird, at the Texaco Trophy

Below: Middlesex captain Mike Gatting gets his muscles stretched by England physiotherapist Bernard Thomas before a Texaco Trophy match

All sweetness and light, Bob Willis, the Warwickshire captain and me before the Benson & Hedges semi-final at Headingley, 20 June. Our loss by 3 runs certainly dispelled my smile (opposite). Here I am coming off during the semi-final

Below: 'Should we bat first? Will Boycs bowl his full 8 overs?' Ted Lester in discussion with me

A stifled appeal: 'No, Boycs, you've already had seven collections on this ground!'

including myself, that let down Yorkshire.

There was still hope when Phil Carrick and Graham Stevenson were batting together at tea. It was a question of accumulating the runs in ones and twos, nothing dramatic or spectacular and, for a while, they appeared to be doing just that. But as the overs ticked away it became apparent that Yorkshire were heading for another catastrophe and that we would be making headlines again the following day, once again for all the wrong reasons.

I said nothing in the silent dressing room afterwards. There was nothing to be added to what had already been said on Tuesday. As I drove home the only consolation I had was the thought that in a way we were paying for our good start to the season.

The cricket world had expected defeats of the size inflicted by Essex and Shropshire to come at the season's start. Instead we had begun well, surprised ourselves and our opponents, and we were now paying for it with a long injury list. We were losing with a team that had to be changed for almost every match. But that didn't alter the fact that we had also played some desperately poor cricket.

I had intended that our players should attend nets at Headingley on the Thursday, only to discover that the nets had been taken down to provide space for the marquees erected during a Test match. I was far from pleased and duly made my feelings known to the members of the Committee.

As I couldn't have a net I found another way of relieving my frustrations – by playing for Parents against the Boys at Fulneck School, Pudsey. The Parents hadn't won for eleven years and our kids, Clare and Andrew, had taken a lot of stick about the Shropshire result.

Anyway I played against the School, sixteen to seventeen year olds, and just about whacked everything. I was told afterwards I hit 10 sixes in my 80 and only ran one single, nearly killing one of the fathers who hadn't taken the precaution of watching which way I was running when I called him for a quick run.

I was eventually run out, but the wicket-keeper got so excited and nervous that he just stood there, grinning at me with the ball in his hand, while I was stranded halfway down the pitch. 'Take the bails off,' I shouted at him – I almost had to do it myself.

It was a great relaxation and, for a while, I could forget the gnawing disappointments of the previous week. Gloucestershire, at Bradford, were our next opponents and my initial step to try to put things right was to order all the first players on the staff, fifteen in all, to Park Avenue on the Saturday morning.

Saturday, 7 July–Tuesday, 10 July

Yorkshire v Gloucestershire
at Bradford

Yorkshire beat Gloucestershire by 8 wickets

This match marked Bill Athey's return to Yorkshire. He was nervous, without admitting it, although those who knew him best in our team recognized his gestures.

We were without Sidebottom and Stevenson, again, but I thought Stuart Fletcher was fit enough to play. We had a long discussion on how we were going to bowl to certain players in Gloucestershire's team. I lost the toss for a change, they batted and got a lot of runs. Four of their first five batsmen, including Athey, topped 50 and Paul Romaines scored 120.

After our disaster at Telford we had called in every

available player to the Park Avenue nets. But Arnie never came into serious contention. I debated whether to play Richard Lumb or Ashley Metcalfe: neither had any first-class runs behind them. In the end I went for Lumb's extra experience, sending him in first with Boycott in the renewal of the regular partnership that has been opening for Yorkshire for the past ten years.

My apprehension about Stuart Fletcher's fitness was well-founded. The lad began the season so well but the strain is now telling in a series of injuries, a pelvic strain, a hip injury. He couldn't perform at all adequately in the Gloucestershire second innings.

Bill Athey scored a century in that Gloucestershire second innings, bringing the total of centuries in the match to five (Romaine, Athey, Boycott, Lumb, Hartley) while John Shepherd and Kevin Sharp should have reached three figures. Richard Lumb reached a career best of 165 not out, while the Athey century, I decided, was destined by Fate, just like Brian Close's at Taunton, in his first game for Somerset against Yorkshire.

Bill looked in good shape, but gave our lads the impression that he was missing Yorkshire. He is a batsman of class and a few people have mentioned to me that it would be nice to have him back in the Yorkshire team again. Where? We have more than enough batsmen. We do need bowlers, urgently. Stuart could be out for some time now and heaven alone knows when we can count on having Sidebottom and Stevenson fully fit again.

We won the match in a run chase following a declaration on the last afternoon, for which Gloucestershire's captain, David Graveney, must have been criticized. Gloucestershire's weakness is similar to our own, they lack sufficient bowlers and the loss of David Lawrence, who split the webbing on his left hand trying to make a catch, proved fatal for them. Had Lawrence bowled, we would not have had 53 overs in which to make the necessary runs, we would have had to take risks in chasing runs, and we might have given Gloucestershire a chance of bowling us out. No captain can take possible injuries into account when timing a declaration.

A few eyebrows were raised when Martyn Moxon appeared as our first slip on the last morning. The fact is that we were short of a good slip; Martyn is our best and, although he was resting his cracked rib, he agreed that the risk was worthwhile. If he had to dive it would be to his right, the rib was on his left side and all in all we both decided the team would benefit. Martyn made one slip catch.

Geoff Boycott passed 45,000 first-class runs on his way to his 142nd century in the Yorkshire second innings, and the Master looked very fit, sharp and in superb form, his century actually coming in only 148 minutes. Yorkshire won by 8 wickets with 17 balls to spare. It was a championship victory that we badly needed to restore spirits after the blows of the previous week. The turning-point in this particular crisis had arrived at Scarborough on the previous Sunday.

Sunday, 8 July

Yorkshire v Gloucestershire

at Scarborough

Yorkshire beat Gloucestershire by 7 wickets

For those who feel that the Yorkshire captain is obsessed with the state of the pitch, I have to explain that there are two factors beyond any cricketer's control that can win or lose a match: the pitch (and I include the weather, which can affect the pitch); and the toss. Being sent in to bat on a difficult surface can cost you a three-day match in an hour.

Scarborough that fine, warm Sunday was a picture. The pitch was one of the best I've ever seen at North Marine Road, white, flat and firm. Ted Lester and I walked out to examine it and I was in a quandary: in a 40-over match I usually prefer to bat second but this surface was so good, how big a risk would that be? There was a large crowd, nearly 10,000. What to do if I won the toss? Ted grinned, 'Lose a few. That will ease the pressure.'

Gloucestershire were put in to bat. I'd decided that Geoff Boycott should open the bowling. He had bowled a great deal the previous year, when we won the John Player League, and I had made up my own mind that if Geoff was going to play a prominent part on a Sunday he would have to bowl. In fact, he bowled an excellent 6 overs for only 16 runs, but kept saying to me, 'He's going to hit, he's going to hit me.'

I replied, perhaps a little testily, 'Boycs, everybody gets hit on a Sunday.'

He was hit for only one four. Bill Athey danced down the wicket and smacked him over long on, the third ball of his sixth over. I could have kicked myself because I had considered, before Geoff bowled that very ball, to stick a man out there.

As I've mentioned before, we had already discussed at length where to bowl at Gloucestershire's batsmen. I had said to young Fletcher, 'Don't bowl at leg or middle to Paul Romaines. That's his strength.' In his second over the lad pitches down the leg side and bangs a four. Next ball, same place, bang, a six. I had to take him off.

I fancied Phil Carrick to block an end, but he neither bowled a length nor full and in line and was swept. We won because Ashley Metcalfe played brilliantly for 115 not out, Yorkshire's first Sunday century for six years, and because he was very well supported by Kevin Sharp.

Sadly the match will not be remembered for Ashley's

91

innings but for the disgusting behaviour of some of the crowd. The two coloured players in Gloucestershire's team, West Indian John Shepherd, an old, valued friend and one of the world's most popular cricketers, and David Lawrence (born in Gloucester!) were jeered and barracked, fruit was thrown, and among the gestures seen were some National Front salutes.

The Yorkshire dressing room was appalled and ashamed but not surprised. We have always felt that if there was to be trouble on any Yorkshire ground it would happen at Scarborough where holidaymakers, who have no interest whatsoever in cricket, know that for admission money of £2 they can drink practically all day on a Sunday.

The Scarborough Club does close the bars between 2.00 and 3.00 p.m., but that is not long enough to sober up people who have been drinking since 12.00, made sure they had full glasses or cans at 2.00 p.m. and then started again at 3.00 p.m.

Unlike Chesterfield, where there was an actual physical clash, the problem got no further than verbal abuse although there could have been violence had either Shepherd or Lawrence reacted. As soon as the match was over, I asked David Hopps of the *Yorkshire Post* to see me and told him, 'All the Yorkshire players are distressed and disgusted at those members of the public on Yorkshire grounds who are picking on coloured players and hurling abuse at them. I am personally apologizing to John Shepherd and David Lawrence.'

I left that apology until the following morning because I felt that the Gloucestershire dressing room wouldn't welcome a stranger in those circumstances. When I did see John Shepherd the following day at Bradford, he accepted the apology but added, 'Bluey, I don't care if I never play cricket in Yorkshire again.'

It was nice to hear the Park Avenue crowd, the following day, give both Lawrence and Shepherd some sympathetic applause, but by then we were back with the three-day game and, of course, among cricket-lovers. Gloucestershire's captain, David Graveney, also spoke to the press the following day, saying, 'I have never played in a game, nor has John Shepherd, for all his experience, where there was so much hostile personal abuse. It's no good blaming it on a mindless minority. The clubs have to find the right balance between the income they receive from the bars and the safety of players, officials and spectators.'

It may be that at Scarborough we are dealing mostly with the ignorant, but I cannot understand the mentality of those so-called Yorkshire cricket supporters who taunt the West Indians. A few years back some idiot is reported to have shouted at Viv Richards at Harrogate when Viv, not too happy with an lbw decision, showed his disapproval with that familiar slow walk back. As he reached the pavilion a voice in the crowd yelled at him, 'You cheating black bastard.' Viv has made Yorkshire pay time and time and time again for that remark.

Why anger West Indian fast bowlers? Yorkshire do not possess a fast bowler now. We cannot retaliate, we just have to grin and bear the bombardment. For every insult we can expect a good score of bouncers around our ears. It's not funny.

Our lads felt especially sorry for young David Lawrence, known on the circuit as 'Syd'. He's a very nice lad, as English as any of us, only twenty years old and, apart from the rights and wrongs of being insulted by ignorant louts on Yorkshire grounds, he can bowl a damn sight quicker than anybody on our side.

It was a sad and sorry affair and left me repeating my warnings to our Committeemen that unless they did get a grip on Sunday licensing hours there would be very serious trouble somewhere on a Yorkshire ground, on a Sunday afternoon, with Scarborough the likely hot spot.

In playing terms we had to think ourselves fortunate to gain two wins over Gloucestershire through our batting strength. As far as our bowling was concerned, we were just patching up from match to match and there seemed no relief in sight. Without our two senior capped seam bowlers, Sidebottom and Stevenson, we were putting too much weight and responsibility on Steve Oldham who, after all, had returned as a bowling coach, and on the youngsters Dennis, Fletcher and Jarvis.

Wednesday, 11 July–Friday, 13 July

Glamorgan v Yorkshire
at Cardiff

Yorkshire drew with Glamorgan

All my accounts of matches seem to start on one of two topics: the pitch, and the state of Arnie Sidebottom's general health and fitness. Sophia Gardens was true to form. The pitch looked damp and the grass had been left on to keep it together. Geoff Boycott agreed with me, 'It will do something for the bowlers.' This was one occasion when I had no choice: Glamorgan sent us in to bat and Greg Thomas gave us a very lively opening spell, bowling as quickly as any English-qualified bowler we met during the season.

We were very pleased to have Arnie back in the team and I was keeping my fingers crossed that this time he would be back to stay. Our initial target was to build up a decent first innings total; when Boycott was lbw to Thomas for 10 at 34, I thought we might be in trouble.

But Lumb and Sharp then stormed away to a stand of 260 in 206 minutes, the highest for any wicket on that ground since Glamorgan moved there from the Arms Park in 1967.

Lumb followed his career best 165 at Bradford with 144 and he looked pretty tired at the end of it. Sharp took his aggregate past 850 for the season and was only seven short of his career best (139) when he played on just after tea. Even I made a few runs and I was able to declare and leave them six overs' batting that evening.

On came Arnie to take a wicket, but he broke down after only two overs and was so depressed we hardly saw him again. He just said, 'Sorry Captain', walked off and refused to join in a traditional visit to a brewery that Yorkshire make when in South Wales. He obviously felt he had let the side down.

The following morning, despite Arnie's absence, at one point we had Glamorgan at 101-5 and seemingly certain to follow on, before their young left-hander, Hugh Morris, came in to score a maiden century. With the help of Rodney Ontong and John Steele he put them pretty well out of danger. Without Arnie we simply didn't have the strength to finish off their first innings.

Simon Dennis (31 overs) and Neil Hartley (32 overs) deserve a mention for all their hard work as Glamorgan batted on. Arnie opened our second innings in order to leave early to visit a specialist, while Geoff Boycott went on to the 143rd century of his career as Glamorgan used nine bowlers. My declaration left them to get 321 in 44 overs so, predictably, the match was drawn.

But I want to stress there was no acrimony between me and the Glamorgan captain, Mike Selvey. I was expecting him to declare once Hugh Morris had scored his 100; that would have given us a lead of 100 with forty minutes to bat that evening. In turn, we would have been able to declare with sufficient time to try to bowl Glamorgan out again. They knew our bowling resources were thin and that Arnie would not be bowling again in the match. They didn't know that Neil Hartley, too, wouldn't be able to bowl again because he had a groin strain after his first innings efforts. I was down to Steve Oldham, who was very tired, Simon Dennis and the two spinners Carrick and Booth.

With our injury situation, I wanted to protect Oldham and Dennis as much as possible, saving them for the weekend fixtures at Lord's. That's why I put myself on to bowl after tea, with Phil Robinson behind the stumps. I wasn't expressing disapproval or 'taking the mickey', just being practical and saving my bowlers.

Glamorgan, in turn, thought they were assisting towards an early declaration by using nine bowlers and were apparently hoping I would set them about six an over. But I was in no position to set them any kind of a target when I didn't have either the time or the bowlers to get them out again. I saw no point in throwing the match away.

The match will be remembered for two facts. First, we all had a laugh at 'Tommy' Hartley's expense. As Lumb and Sharp piled up their double hundred Neil sat with his pads on, saying every now and then, 'After a big stand there is always somebody who fails.' He lost his off stump, sweeping at the third ball he received, and he was so furious with himself that I fully expected him to return not to the pavilion but to a green van where two white men would have been waiting with straitjackets.

The other development was less funny, but not unexpected. I was travelling with Richard Lumb, who told me that he would not be seeking a new contract, that he had already sold his house, and that he would be emigrating to South Africa at the end of the season. He added, 'Had you been captain two years ago, Stanley, my decision might have been different. I almost didn't come back from South Africa last winter but I felt I did owe it you to return and finish off the contract.'

He filled in one or two gaps in my knowledge of the factors that led up to my captaincy. Despite Ray Illingworth's statement that I had sulked because Lumb had been offered the captaincy, Richard had made it plain that he never wanted the job. He thought he may have been used. I agreed. I think Lumb, a player good enough to have opened for England, was a victim of circumstance in Yorkshire's power struggle.

Something else he said also confirmed what I had suspected: if the former committee had retained power and sacked Geoff Boycott, the next player to go could have been David Bairstow.

Saturday, 14 July

Interlude: Stormy

Today the Yorkshire Post *published an interview with Gail. I wasn't too happy at the thought of what had to be at least a minor intrusion into our private lives, but Gail was keen to tell her story and, as everyone knows, I always win arguments with my wife. This is the interview, written by Roger Cross, and reproduced by courtesy of the Editor:*

> Gail Bairstow approaches life in the same way her flame-haired husband tackles cricket as captain of Yorkshire, and sometimes keeper of the stumps for England. She leads with her chin and doesn't duck the bouncers.
>
> She may sway away from the odd full-toss these days, but as her husband tends to worry each match by the throat, so his vivacious and tempestuous wife is a natural front foot attacking player in the game of living.
>
> As such she has become almost as legendary a part of the Yorkshire cricket scene for these last dozen years as her famous husband. If the average cricket fan has never heard of her, or even heard her, it is not because she has cultivated a low profile.
>
> And if some of the old guard Yorkshire aficionados, not to mention committee members. seemed pained during the Boycott

upheaval, there were those who positively winced when David 'Bluey' Bairstow was made captain nine months ago.

For along with the tough and combative former Bradford Hanson Boys' Grammar School sporting boy prodigy came Gail, a legend in her own lunchbreak, tea interval, and often the bits in between.

Her often caustic wit and ever-ready opinions on, in and around the Yorkshire and England teams, sometimes helped on their way into the world by the demon drink, have not endeared her to all.

It has even been suggested that her over-the-top approach cost David Bairstow a place on the last England tour to Australia.

It is not known whether Lord Hawke's wife turned in her grave on October 4 last year, or even what Lady Dorothy Hutton was thinking in Surrey suburbia. But from that day Yorkshire cricket got a captain's wife the likes of which it had never seen before.

Her husband's impact as leader has been impressive, with the team healthily placed in the County Championship after the ignominy of finishing bottom last year. Bairstow's heroics almost snatched a place for Yorkshire in the Benson and Hedges final at Lords.

"They were three runs short of Warwickshire's total and when Bluey [a nickname bestowed by the Australians] woke up the following morning he was almost suicidal, so disappointed and depressed."

Gail Bairstow's inspired answer was to invite all the other players and their wives to a barbecue that afternoon, a free day from cricket, at their lovely Georgian home at Gomersal. "It was my treat, my way of bucking them up. It seemed to work and by the end of the day David was his old self," she recalls.

It is hard to imagine the lionhearted Bairstow being subdued about anything for long. He refused to be beaten when he first saw Gail working as a beauty consultant at Brown Muff's in Bradford in 1973. She bowled him a googly but he spotted it.

"He had a broken nose and long hair and he loved himself. He was so ugly I thought he was punch-drunk, but he had such lovely manners. He still has. He just walked up to me and asked

me out. I wasn't keen so I said I would but planned to send my friend instead."

The then 21-year-old Bairstow, a Yorkshire regular for three years and a highly rated footballer with Bradford City at the time, foiled her plan by calling unexpectedly at her Liversedge home.

That was in February 1973, and they were married on the following August 31 so she could go with Bairstow as his wife on a winter coaching assignment to South Africa.

"David was a bit of a prude about that sort of thing; he still is. He insists that everything is above board. He can't stand hypocrisy. Mind you being a typical Yorkshireman he likes to look at girls in mini-skirts but won't let me wear them," she says with a laugh.

He had insisted on their first date he was going to marry her but Gail Lesley Dobson had not been so sure. "I can't pretend ours has been a wonderfully romantic relationship. We are both very strong willed and have been awful to each other at times, but it has worked, particularly in the last few years," she offers with refreshing candour.

Since Bairstow was appointed captain, Gail has kept her head down more, conscious of her new responsibilities. She knew he was uneasy about her talking to us.

Professional sportsmen are used to specialist sports writers concentrating almost exclusively, and conveniently, on on-field activities, often turning a blind eye to off-field indiscretions.

When Gail Bairstow went out with other England wives to join the 1979/80 tour to Australia for five weeks, she candidly admits she was the worse for drink before boarding the plane. Twenty-four, mainly riotous, hours later she was still tottering at Sydney airport. "I would have been wiser to stick to Perrier water," she reflects wryly.

Gail Bairstow was never an alcoholic but concedes she drank too much at cricket matches. "A few before lunch, some wine with lunch, and then there was the afternoon. It was never out of my system, really.

"I enjoyed it but sometimes I went over the top. The drink made me stupid and I said things I wouldn't dream of saying sober. I go bright red just thinking about it now."

Her deepest shade of beetroot is reserved for a verbal assault she made on Fred Trueman's wife at a one-day international four years ago. "It was cold, I had only had a salad for lunch, and plenty of wine. I felt Fred had insulted me the night before and I said something dreadful to his wife. I was wrong and it will live with me forever."

After Bairstow's record-breaking £56,000 benefit year they went to Hawaii for a winter holiday and Gail overdid it at a cocktail party with some Americans they had met. "I couldn't get out of bed in the morning and felt so awful I vowed I would never drink again."

That was 18 months ago in Honolulu and she has kept her promise to herself and says her life has changed radically as a result.

"David never criticised me and has always been very supportive but I know he is pleased. Everyone who cares about me is."

Indeed there are those who say that decision cleared the way, inadvertently, for her husband to succeed some of Yorkshire cricket's greatest legends as captain of the proudest county nine months later.

Yet there are many close to Yorkshire cricket who see her as one of Bairstow's greatest assets: Someone to match his strong will, equally ambitious for him and the Yorkshire team, a pragmatist in an often unreal world.

Her willingness here to dust down a few skeletal cupboard dwellers will surprise only those of a nervous or ostrich-like disposition. "David is always open and honest and I try to be the same. There is no point in pretending you are not less than perfect."

So did she think she had hindered his England career? "I know it has been suggested that I have not done David any good, that he was left out of the tour to Australia because I didn't get on with the other England wives. I don't believe it.

"If he really has been punished because of me, then he will never go on tour again because there is no way he would drop me. I admit I have been probably too outspoken in the past but I

100

think people have got it wrong."

Her admiration for Bairstow as a cricketer is undiminished and she enjoys the beautiful Georgian home with its five bedrooms and two bathrooms his feats have produced. Their two children are privately educated.

She believes equally passionately 'Bluey' should be in the England Test team. She won't be at Headingley today to watch them play the West Indies.

"I hope England do well, but it will be no place for an England has-been wife," she says with a chuckle. RIP Lady Hawke.

Sunday, 15 July

Middlesex v Yorkshire

at Lord's

Middlesex beat Yorkshire by 7 wickets

There had been no play on the Saturday, when the championship match was due to start, because the ground was unfit for play. The ends of the Test match pitch had been left uncovered and were solid mud. Had it happened on any other ground in the country there would have been a serious row, but as it's Lord's will anyone take any notice? Will it be reported? If it is reported, will the Test and County Cricket Board rap Middlesex and MCC?

The only reason I could discover why the ground should be in such a state was that MCC and Scotland had continued playing in rain during the previous match. Would that excuse be accepted elsewhere? What would have been said and done about Abbeydale, for instance, if the ground had been unfit because Sheffield Collegiate had continued to play on during rain?

The uncovered ends also meant that we couldn't start play on the Sunday until 3.45 p.m., when they were put under matting to allow the match to get under way in very poor light. We had only 25 overs to bat and simply didn't make enough runs – had we reached 150 we would have set them a run a ball, but 132 was a comparatively easy task for them.

Mike Gatting hit 35 in 6 overs to kill off our chances and, with them, any remaining hope we had of retaining the John Player Championship. He might have been caught by Kevin Sharp at deep square leg but the light was so poor Kevin never actually saw the ball. When Gatting was out, Middlesex needed only 27 in 6 overs to win.

The light didn't help our batting either (a topic I have good reason to return to shortly) and we had to be grateful to Metcalfe, Hartley and Carrick for holding our innings together.

Our bowling was so weakened that we had called up a twenty-year-old lad from Heckmondwike in the Yorkshire Central League, who had been taking wickets regularly for the second team. His name is Chris Shaw and, considering all the circumstances, he performed very creditably. To be thrown into a Sunday game of reduced overs, still keep length and line, and at Lord's, would be a severe test for anyone. He conceded only 26 runs in his 5 overs and I was very pleased with him.

In a match of reduced overs it is essential that you get after the opposition's fifth bowler. Few sides can afford to carry a fifth bowler or a genuine all-rounder and you have to chase that one when he appears. Middlesex got after our fifth: Neil Hartley was hit for 32 off 21 balls. We didn't chase Wilf Slack enough (1-28 in his 5 overs). It's on as fine a margin as this that one-day matches are decided.

Middlesex v Yorkshire
at Lord's

Middlesex beat Yorkshire by 9 wickets

In a match reduced to two days, our first of the season, it was essential to field first because otherwise there wasn't time to bowl a side out twice. Not that we had a strong enough attack to bowl out any team inside two days but I opted for the extra batsman, intending to use Neil Hartley again as our extra bowler.

I lost the toss. We were sent in and were fortunate that Wayne Daniel had to withdraw through injury and Neil Williams made a delayed appearance because of hospital treatment to a damaged finger. That meant that we had to face, in the gloom at the start, only one black fast bowler.

Lumb lost his middle stump to Norman Cowans. Then Williams came into the attack, taking a wicket in each of his first three overs on a pitch on which the bounce was certainly variable. Metcalfe was caught behind playing a millionaire's shot, while Kevin Sharp and Hartley were both out lbw.

When Cowans returned he had Boycott caught hooking at a bumper. When I faced him I had just about time to realize that the ball was worn and blending into the red of the pavilion, that I had to pick up a black arm in poor light, and that people were moving about on either side of the screen. I never saw the ball that hit me.

I just felt the crack on the left side of the helmet. I didn't go down, just walked about until Clive Radley came across and said, 'You'll have to go off. You're cut.'

Somehow the time stuck in my mind. It was 12.45. The ball had cracked into the part of the helmet that protects the ears, driving it into my cheek. I remember thinking, over and over, 'That's frightening. I never saw the ball leave "Flash's" hand.' Then Clive Radley said, 'There's a lump coming up.' Umpire Don Oslear also came up, took one look and declared, 'Off you go. You can't stay on with that.'

I remember being ushered off, then driven to hospital after John Miller, the Middlesex physiotherapist had given me a preliminary examination and made the arrangements. The doctor was a Lancastrian. He examined my jaw and head and came to the conclusion that there wasn't a fracture. But I began to bleed from the left ear and to feel dizzy.

I was patched up with a big pad over my ear, but I knew that there was no question of playing again in the match. Every time I put my head down it seemed to go round and round and while I was walking about I would feel dizzy every now and again, a sensation that persisted for days and led to my own doctor ordering the week's rest I had refused during the Essex match.

I spent the rest of that match doing 12th man duties, helped by a friend, knowing that I was out of cricket until my head felt right again. Later that day I saw the great Keith Miller and he made a very succinct comment, 'It's always been bad batting from that end. I'm surprised something like this has not happened before.'

Yorkshire tried hard to hang on through the Tuesday after Middlesex had run up 303-8 declared. Our bowling was just too young and inexperienced to contain Middlesex but Shaw, with 4–68 off 20 overs, again emerged from the fire with credit.

Neil Hartley hung on for 56 overs and 54 runs and with Phil Carrick added 68 in 35 overs. Not very entertaining stuff but at least we worried Middlesex enough to make them wonder if they had time to win and that, in itself, was an achievement in all the circumstances.

Wednesday, 17 July

Interlude: Dizzy

Ordered to rest, I watched the Benson & Hedges final on television yesterday. I was very pleased for John Abrahams of Lancashire who, like myself, is in his first season as captain of a county that is under tremendous pressure to succeed. He's managed it and good luck to him. My thoughts are so obvious I feel a little embarrassed to record them: I should have been at Lord's, in John's place, holding up that Benson & Hedges Trophy. Up till last season, when we did win the John Player League, I had reconciled myself to the thought that I might never win anything with Yorkshire. This season I am very conscious of the fact that we came so close to beating Warwickshire twice, and should have beaten them, and thus could have been in their place at Lord's. Having got that far, I think it would have taken more than Lancashire to have stopped us.

But I have to be positive. We have achieved far more than most people expected and there were several members of the old committee waiting to jump, waiting to say, 'No wicket-keeper has ever captained a successful side.'

I've no personal regrets about trying to do both jobs. I've had terrific support from the team and while a captain has his team behind him he doesn't have too much to fear. The spirit is very high. At Lord's, when I was all but knocked out, I was told very firmly by several senior members of the team that I had to take a rest. 'No one could have done more than you have this season. Don't kill yourself' was the gist of the message.

I know there are rumours, one being that Geoff Boycott would like to be captain again. He has denied that to me. I think he now fancies himself as manager rather than captain. He once said to me, 'With me as manager and you as captain we could do a Clough and Taylor for Yorkshire.'

What the team do not want, and I can say this with complete confidence, is Boycott to take charge with the attitudes he had when he was captain. He will treat the kids as though they can see the game in the same way as he can, after all his experience. They can't, of course; a resentment builds up and the team starts to fracture.

At the moment, despite our setbacks, things are going reasonably well. We recognize our weaknesses and we must rectify them. The team is sound, we believe in what we are doing and if we can get a couple of players fit we can start winning championship points again.

Yorkshire have been knocked out of two one-day competitions and after our defeat at the hands of Middlesex we have to accept that we cannot retain the John Player League Trophy. What we have to do now is ensure that we finish in a respectable position in the county championship.

What we also have to do, before very much longer, is to have a long, hard think about our seam bowlers. We cannot continue to throw in kids like cannon fodder. Simon Dennis, despite his cap, Paul Jarvis, Stuart Fletcher and

Chris Shaw are all still apprentices. Steve Oldham has done far more than should be expected of a veteran. He is, after all, supposed to be the bowling coach. Arnie Sidebottom has bowled his heart out when fit, but it's very clear that if we are to get the best out of him he has to be used in short spells; we cannot use him as a stock bowler. That leaves Graham Stevenson, whom we have hardly seen in championship cricket this year. Much as I love Stevo, the fact has to be faced that his career is at the crossroads. He has got to prove to the club and to me that he has sufficient dedication to the job if he wants to continue being a Yorkshire player.

What are the alternatives? We have to find at least one experienced seam bowler before next season, and with that in mind I intend to propose that Yorkshire make an approach to Neal Mallender of Northants at the end of his contract. Neal is Hull-born and therefore qualified to play for Yorkshire. He's only twenty-three but experienced and could do a great job for us over the next few years. Long term, I am inclined to the view that if Yorkshire are to compete fully again they will have to abandon the birthright policy and sign an overseas star. And I know one who would be delighted to come.

Hampshire v Yorkshire
at Bournemouth

Hampshire beat Yorkshire by 31 runs

This was the first time I had missed a Yorkshire first-team match because of injury in fourteen years. It was strange to be at home when the team were playing and I felt restless until I began to perform one of my regular chores of winter, preparing the vegetables for lunch.

We had some friends around for a traditional Sunday dinner but I couldn't forget what was going on at Bournemouth. I rang Ted Lester to find out what was happening before the match began, and all through the afternoon I was switching on Ceefax to keep up with the score. Needless to add, I was very disappointed when they lost, and gathered subsequently that if a couple of silly run-outs hadn't occurred Yorkshire would have had a good chance of winning.

Chris Shaw will certainly remember the match. He is twenty, an apprentice electrician with the National Coal Board (he had no difficulties in getting time off this summer!) and up to a few weeks ago was happily playing Central Yorkshire League cricket with Heckmondwike. The high casualty rate among the senior team bowlers meant that he was called into the second team where he

108

started taking wickets: he's tall with an easy run, medium fast, with good control for his age and experience.

More injuries meant that he had to be given a first-team chance perhaps a year too soon, and this occasion was his second Sunday match. He took 5-41, which was the best return by a Yorkshire bowler in this competition for two years and came when sorely needed, for Geoff Boycott, leading the team, was without Sidebottom, Stevenson, Fletcher and Oldham. Thanks to young Chris, a Hampshire total of 233-9 was not unbeatable. It could have been much worse, for Hampshire were 221-3 in the 36th over, Mark Nicholas having hit 94 which included sixes off Boycott and Simon Dennis.

Yorkshire began badly again, losing Moxon, Boycott and Metcalfe for 15, but Kevin Sharp kept Yorkshire in the game with a very bright 74 off 84 deliveries. Neil Hartley gave him some stout support, also giving Nicholas some stick, and the disappointments came with the running out of Carrick and Robinson when, for the first time, it seemed possible Yorkshire would pull off a surprising win.

Why, I was asked several times, were Yorkshire sending in their opponents when Yorkshire's bowling, quite clearly, wasn't strong enough to bowl them out cheaply?

I had hoped that we could bowl tightly and accurately enough to restrict the opposition to around 300 while we picked up a few wickets in the first 100 overs. Our target would then be 300 in the 100 overs, seeking as many bonus points as possible. This would give the opposition a small lead and we hoped that, if they wanted to win the match, we would get a sporting declaration and, if we batted well enough, the chance of victory. I have to admit that I just could not see Yorkshire bowling a side out twice.

There's one lesson you learn quickly as a captain: whatever may have to be said for various reasons to the team, to the committee, to the media, to your friends, and to your wife, the one person you cannot keep the truth from regarding the form, fitness, morale and capabilities of you and your players is yourself.

Interlude: Dizzy revisited

A special meeting of the club's Cricket Sub-Committee was held today. I was asked to report at Headingley at 9 a.m. but no reason was given either for the suddenness of the meeting or for the early hour.

Last night I got a call from Graham Stevenson. He had also been asked to appear before the committee at noon. He asked, 'Do you know what it's all about?'

I replied, 'I haven't a clue.'

There was a little laughing and joking and then he asked, 'Are they going to give me my cards?' He meant that as another joke, but underneath I could sense that the lad was worried.

He hadn't played for a while, his figures had not been good when he had played, and with the team's results also fading I think he feared that there might be a temptation among some members of the committee to look for a scapegoat, a sacrifice to appease the wrath of the public. My own feelings on Graham were well known: he is an England player who has to be convinced, sometimes, that he is good enough to be a professional cricketer.

I arrived at Headingley, joined the sub-committee (meeting in the Leeds Rugby League club boardroom), drank a cup of coffee and discussed the situation with Brian Close (the chairman), Phil Sharpe (also an England selector), Tony Vann (who represents the new element), Tony Woodhouse and Jack Sokell, the last two of whom were members of the old committee but who were inclined to be pro- rather than anti-Boycott.

Committee business is, of course, confidential and I would not reveal it, but I'm not breaking any confidences when I say that the basic discussion was about the number and extent of injuries to players and what effect they had on the team's performances. The mystery of that meeting was that no explanation was offered as to the absence of Bob Appleyard, who had been specially co-opted on to that committee and asked to help with the bowling coaching.

I left the meeting intending to have a net, only to find that none was available, so the Yorkshire captain had to knock up on the boundary edge. I wore a helmet because I was still a little worried about my injured head. Steve Oldham, who was feeling a groin strain, helped by bowling at two stumps. Graham Stevenson, in civvies, joined in as soon as he arrived and I was also helped by Paul Jarvis, also in civvies.

I was annoyed that there were no nets for practice and even more annoyed to find that Paul, who is nineteen, was stuck in a hotel round the corner from Headingley. He lives in Marske, up near Redcar, and it is obviously impossible for him to travel every day when Yorkshire are playing south of Harrogate or Scarborough. But I do not believe that it is a good thing for a lad to be stuck in a hotel on his own; he needs companionship, something like a family life. I felt sad for him.

Stevenson was called before the committee just before noon. He saw both Brian Close and the club chairman, Reg Kirk. I don't know what happened and it would be wrong for me to speculate.

My own problem was finding a team to play

Worcestershire at Scarborough. Even though Jim Love had scored a century for the second team and was a capped player, I felt I had to stand by my original selection and back Philip Robinson as a gesture of appreciation for his performances in previous championship games. He had played so much better than anyone could possibly have anticipated, remembering he had arrived as a twenty-year-old straight out of Bradford League cricket. Whichever combination I tried I knew I would be back to a team that, four elder statesmen apart, would look rather like Yorkshire schoolboys when they took the field. There were times when I would cast a glance round the dressing room and feel tempted to dig out my own old, faded Yorkshire schoolboys' cap to wear and to turn back the years.

All this is no reflection on Philip Robinson, Paul Jarvis, Paul Booth (eighteen), Ian Swallow (twenty-two), Ashley Metcalfe (twenty), Stuart Fletcher (twenty), and Steven Rhodes (twenty) – as you can see, there were occasions when Yorkshire were at only one-third strength, not even half strength.

All the 'schoolboys' showed plenty of character. It would be too much to expect all of them to survive and become capped players themselves one day, but I had a great deal of quiet satisfaction in thinking to myself that each one of them had a chance of becoming a Yorkshire player, and several had the ability to be prospective Test players.

I set off for Scarborough on a beautiful sunny evening. After the humidity inland, the fresh sparkle of the sea air was a delight and I felt my spirits rise as soon as I arrived. Scarborough on a clear day puts a tingle in the blood that is found nowhere south of Skegness, but then I'm biased.

I was walking across from the team's hotel to the Royal Hotel to see my co-author when I heard someone shout 'Bluey'. A luxurious dark blue Mercedes saloon drew alongside. The driver was a grinning Kapil Dev. India's captain wanted to know where his Worcestershire colleagues were staying and how to find his way to the North Marine Road ground. I passed on the information,

112

exchanged a joke or two with Kapil and his beautiful wife, and then thought to myself, as he drove away, with not a little envy, 'There must be some riches in winning the World Cup.'

Yorkshire v Worcestershire
at Scarborough

Yorkshire drew with Worcestershire

When I arrived at North Marine Road this morning I was trying to conceal the fact that I was still very worried about the crack on my head. I didn't feel right. I had my helmet on in the nets but I couldn't get my feet moving properly and I was expecting to be hit on the head all the time. I was very concerned. Even when I sat in the pavilion I took the easy option by sending in Phil Carrick to bat before me. I felt I needed every possible minute to give myself time to get right.

'You're not passing the buck,' I told myself. 'You haven't had a run in first-class cricket for a long time. Fergie is in better nick than you are. It's only right he should go in at number six.' I convinced myself that this was wise.

There was never any question of our batting second on what I expected to be a slow turner, and accordingly we found ourselves in deep trouble although the actual toss-up, with Worcestershire captain Phil Neale, gave me a hearty laugh. When I told him we would bat he pretended to glance round the terraces in some alarm and then

113

whispered; 'What time can we expect them to start throwing bananas?'

Boycott agreed with me that we should bat first, yet I had a premonition of trouble. It was one of those occasions when I somehow felt I was making the wrong decision even though I knew I was right! My head said we would bat all day and get 400 and plenty, and my sixth sense said, 'You're going to get rolled over' . . . and we very nearly were.

I know I was in a curious mood today. On the one hand I was elated because I had managed to come back to play, worried though I might be about my own fitness. On the other hand I was incensed by a quote from Norman Cowans who apparently said that the ball that hit me at Lord's was too quick for me. All I could reply to that was that I have played against much quicker bowlers than Norman Cowans.

I did feel as though I knew my own mind. I'd told Arnie Sidebottom to report to Scarborough for a net. Afterwards he thought he was ready to play but I wasn't risking another Glamorgan débâcle. I told him to rest, have treatment and bowl in the nets for three days. When Arnie comes back this time I want him to stay in the side.

Phil Neale wanted to bat first but must have been pleased he bowled. Martyn Moxon was out first ball and felt sick about it; he squeezed out a near yorker and gave second slip a hard, low catch. Sharp was caught off bat and pad, Hartley, who has been playing better than most, didn't move his feet properly and was caught on the pads, Robinson was caught behind off a ball that 'snaked' at him, and Boycott got a similar delivery.

So I arrived, not in the best frame of mind, at 24–5. I hit the first ball over extra cover for 4, after arriving at the crease with no special intention of playing aggressively. Yet immediately I felt a surge of confidence and form; it was like having new blood pumped through me. My doubts began to fade, although I was very conscious that Worcestershire must be thinking, 'He's bound to be nervous of a bouncer after just being hit on the head.'

114

Oddly enough it wasn't my head I was concerned about by the end of the innings; it was my back. I struck John Inchmore for three fours in one over and when I hit the third, through midwicket, I felt a muscle pull on the right side of my back. I'd been having treatment on my back all season after some chill I picked up on one of those cold days in May. Now I knew I had another problem, and our physio spotted it immediately. As soon as I played the shot he ran to the edge of the field, saying to the dressing room, 'That's it. His back's gone.' It was a brilliant piece of instant diagnosis; all I knew was that I would have great difficulty in keeping wicket in their innings. I decided that, for the next few days, I would have to take the field with a Heineken bar towel strapped across my lower abdomen.

Of course, I was sorry to miss my century and even sorrier to be last out, but I received a nice compliment from Ted Lester who thought it was one of the best innings, for timing the ball, he had ever seen me play.

The main point about Worcestershire's innings, and we didn't have much luck when it came to hanging on to edges – and also, it must be admitted, dropped three catches – was Paul Jarvis's career-best 6-115. Some time in the last three weeks Paul has turned from a boy to a young man.

Jarvis was the youngest player ever to appear for Yorkshire (sixteen years and seventy-five days in 1981) and was immediately hailed as the player around whom the new attack was built. That was too much for any boy, and for a couple of seasons he seemed to go backwards. Then, just recently, he has started to volunteer, 'I'll bowl, captain,' when we are going through a sticky patch. He asked to go in recently as night-watchman.

I can't take credit for advising him to cut down his run. Perhaps it was joint advice. Certainly we noticed he was bowling straighter and quicker off a shorter run. I do remember telling him that when Chris Old was younger and a genuine fast-medium bowler he had realized that the preamble to his run, some five or six paces, could be cut to two or three without losing either rhythm or speed. Steve

115

Oldham has had a few chats with the lad and the results have been impressive.

With Jarvis finding form, Stuart Fletcher about to return to net bowling, the discovery of Chris Shaw, and the approaching fitness of both Arnie Sidebottom and Graham Stevenson, I feel that I can almost see daylight again. We may soon be able to return Steve Oldham to his proper job of coaching the youngsters: he will have to take a good look at Simon Dennis, who has had such a disappointing season after leading the attack last year and winning his cap. Yet Jarvis still has some way to go. He has this habit of running up and just letting the ball go. He's got to learn commitment, to put his body into every delivery, really to bang in the ball. When he can do that consistently we shall have a truly hostile young seamer.

For several reasons, Paul Jarvis being one of them, Worcestershire rather lost their way. Against our attack and against a wicket-keeper with a bad back, they should have made more runs more quickly. However, Phil Neale no doubt felt he had Yorkshire on the run.

I must also mention Paul Booth's performance with bat and ball. In his first season he's had about eight catches dropped off his bowling and he nearly raised a 100 stand with me. He's a kid making his way in a man's world and I've felt very proud of him, even if I did have to call him a 'silly little bugger' during that Scarborough innings.

'Don't hook,' I told him. 'They're faster than you think.' My mind went back to my first innings against Mike Procter, at Bradford. I expected Procter's bouncer to reach me at about the same speed as bouncers in the Bradford League. It wasn't. It hit me. It hurt.

So when young Paul tried to hook Kapil and got pinged on the glove I shouted, 'What did I tell you? Don't hook.'

'It was impulse,' he said. 'I couldn't help it.' Damn me if he didn't try it again and got a ball right on the glove. This time he was hurt.

'You silly little bugger,' I yelled. 'How many more times do I have to tell you?'

He grimaced and grinned. He'll try again, I know. He'll learn how to do it properly as I did, with flattened knuckles and bruised chest and the real sickener, when you lose sight of it, duck, and it bombs into the helmet. You pray that whatever damage is done won't be serious and won't put you out of the match.

One of the mysteries and statistical gems of this particular match was that Geoffrey Boycott did not face the first ball in either innings. No one could remember the last time that had happened in a championship match in Yorkshire; it was probably the first occasion in twenty years.

What happened in the first innings was that we were informed that Worcestershire would bowl the first innings from the Press Box End, uphill, and Boycott accordingly went to face from that end. Then Worcestershire changed their minds, Kapil Dev came downhill from the Trafalgar Square end, and had Moxon out first ball.

Martyn made up for it in the second innings with a splendid 126 not out, restarting the stampede to get him into the England side, albeit at the expense of the unlucky Paul Terry. I still wish they would leave him alone, at least until the Sri Lanka Test. Boycott, in the meantime, had aggravated a groin strain and dropped down the order in the same innings. He would have batted only in an emergency which, thanks to the batting of Moxon and Philip Robinson and the Friday afternoon rain, never materialized.

Yorkshire v Leicestershire
at Sheffield

Yorkshire drew with Leicestershire

Abbeydale is a name that haunts Yorkshire captains, as readers of this journal will appreciate. To say that the pitch has been 'indifferent' over the years is a euphemism. You never know what to expect. What does seem to have happened is that the groundsman, fed up with years of criticism, has settled for a bland surface on which a draw is the most likely result. It happened again in this match, although there could have been a result.

Leicestershire had been among the championship leaders all season, but we met them when David Gower and Nick Cook were absent with England and when both their West Indian fast bowlers, one of whom could have played, were recovering from injury. 'I only wish I had Andy Roberts or George Ferris to bowl down that slope,' was one remark made by Leicestershire's acting captain, Peter Willey. Where would some counties be without their overseas professionals?

Yorkshire were starting to return to normal. We had Martyn Moxon back, Arnie Sidebottom was returning, and Graham Stevenson would be fit for the Sunday game. Jim Love had returned to his regular spot in the middle of the order. My back was still troubling me and I prayed to win the toss so I could give it a longer rest. At such times, of course, the toss is lost. Leicestershire went in to bat and we dropped four or five catches that made all the difference.

They, in turn, scored 237-4 which I thought, in all the circumstances, should have been 450-9, but they were no doubt pleased with their day because we had lost both Boycott and Moxon before the close.

I had deliberately gone for the extra batsman, regretting that I had to disappoint either Simon Dennis or Chris Shaw and knowing I was putting a lot of responsibility on Neil Hartley as the third seamer.

By Monday morning we were struggling and were rescued from a possible follow-on by the grit and resolution of Jim Love. When he had scored 30 he was hit on the hand by Leicestershire's Hull-born Australian left-arm fast-medium bowler, Ian Carmichael. Jim went on batting for another ninety minutes, to reach 84, with a broken little finger on his left hand.

Kevin Sharp passed 1,000 runs in a season for the first time in his career and also, in the same match, took his first first-class wicket. 'Did you get a picture?' he asked a photographer afterwards, hopefully.

There was a typical Yorkshire reply, 'Aye, of the slater replacing tiles on that roof where they kept hitting you.'

Assessing our bowling performances against Worcestershire and Leicestershire I took comfort from the fact that, although we had conceded a lot of runs, we never got slogged and we were always able to exert some measure of control. Heads never dropped and dressing-room spirits remained high. In fact, with a hyper-critical public to please, I wasn't unhappy with the way the team had recovered from that awful week of Essex and Telford. While injuries continued to handicap the side, we couldn't expect any dramatic victories, but there was a silver lining: the young lads were being tested very early in their careers and the results were promising.

Peter Willey eventually set us to score 290 to win in 66

overs which, as the Press declared, was a reasonable target. There was a little variable bounce in the pitch, but as the Abbeydale square is on a slope it is not an easy ground upon which to defend the boundaries.

As we were without our fastest scoring specialist batsman, Jim Love, and could bat only ten, I think Peter Willey used the wrong tactics. He had to risk losing 16 points. Yorkshire were not in contention for the championship, so that conceding 16 points was immaterial, and I think he made the error of trying to bowl us out.

Boycott made a good point. He referred back to the 1960s when Yorkshire won the championship regularly under Brian Close, 'Closey made some ridiculous declarations on the third day, putting the opposition in such a situation that they had to keep chasing the runs. Yorkshire won many a match that way.'

Leicestershire bowled so well, and fielded so accurately, that by the time they brought on Chris Balderstone to lob up a few balls Yorkshire were so far behind the clock that all that was left was survival. Strange tactics because a draw was as bad as a defeat to Leicestershire: they couldn't win unless they gave us a chance to win.

Yorkshire v Leicestershire
at Bradford

Yorkshire won by 1 run

One ball to go, 2 runs wanted, Leicestershire wicket-keeper Mike Garnham facing Neil Hartley. That was the finale!

Bradford is my home town and Park Avenue my home ground, and the crowd have always been kind to me. But there's no doubt they are the most fickle and two-faced of any of the Yorkshire crowds. The mood can change as quickly as a model changes costumes in a fashion parade. Is it the sun? Or the booze? You tell me. I can't work them out. As I say, I've always been treated as a local lad but at least two of our players, Richard Lumb and Jim Love, have never felt they could please Park Avenue.

This particular afternoon the comments were flying thick and fast until that electric last over when, you might say, Garnham snatched defeat from the jaws of victory.

I had lost the toss and we were sent in to bat and scored 230, a satisfactory performance. When Leicestershire came in to bat we exchanged a little banter with Ian Butcher, who had scored an incredibly lucky century on the Saturday. I had said to Boycott, 'You couldn't call Butch's innings a classic, could you? Compared with one of yours it was the *Beano* to a play by William Shakespeare.'

121

He laughed, and enjoyed the compliment. Then the very first ball that Graham Stevenson bowled to Butcher flew off the edge and I called up to the batsman, 'You've been to church again, Butch.'

One of the absolute rules of one-day cricket is never to leave your best bowler unbowled, in other words to make sure that he does his full stint. With that in mind I brought Arnie Sidebottom back for a middle spell to balance Steve Oldham's worst Sunday figures since he returned to Yorkshire.

I told Neil Hartley he would have to bowl the last three; it was perhaps a little unfair on a non-specialist but he responded magnificently. Leicestershire, needing 20 off the last 18 balls with 6 wickets in hand, ought to have won by a mile but we put the pressure on and fought for every run. Phil Carrick said to me, 'Are you confident?'

I replied, 'I'm backing Yorkshire,' but I don't think I had many supporters in the crowd at that moment.

Before Neil could bowl the last ball – 2 runs wanted, remember – Garnham suddenly sat down and decided to adjust a shoelace. Whether it was nerves or a delaying tactic I do not know, but it gave us a chance to talk to Neil. He asked Boycott and me, 'Are we going for a win or a tie?'

Geoff said instantly, 'Go for a tie and you might get a win.'

I said, 'I'm backing you to bowl him. He's unlikely to hit the last ball straight – he'll try to swing across the line for two.'

Cricket, of course, is magically unpredictable. I expected Neil to put one in the blockhole, Garnham to swing and probably miss, and the pole to be knocked out. But Garnham drove the ball back virtually straight, Neil flung himself to stop the ball with his left, turned on the pitch and threw down the stumps before Garnham could complete the run.

You would have thought the ground would have been in uproar. There was certainly a cheer but nothing like such a win deserved. I think we had stunned a crowd ready to give

122

us some stick as we left the field. But there was no shortage of cheer and laughter in the dressing room. And champagne from chairman Reg Kirk.

I heard Douglas Jardine in a television documentary quoting an un-named New Zealander, 'Cricket is battle and service and sport and art.' I'll remember that.

Saturday, 4 August–Tuesday, 7 August

Lancashire v Yorkshire
at Old Trafford

Lancashire drew with Yorkshire

A bad weather forecast turned out to be all too correct. More rain, more delays and, as usual at Old Trafford, the umpires and John Abrahams and I had to put up with a barrage of heckling every time we went to and from the square for an inspection. 'Come on, get on with it' and 'When are you going to start?', the last in a surly, aggressive tone, were the most polite contributions.

I don't know why the Old Trafford members should make so much fuss. Seated where they are, square on to the pitch, they can't have much idea of what's going on, anyway. The same point had been made during the Test match against West Indies when Matthew Engel, in the *Guardian*, noted that the best view on the ground had been given to the occupants of the new executive boxes, 'most of whom wouldn't know mid on from a maraschino cherry'.

Prospects were hopeless on that Saturday. The very

heavy overnight rain had left minor swamps all over the square, and it was obvious from the very start that there was no chance of play until there had been a long drying-out period. But we hung on and hung on, because it was Old Trafford and a Roses match and there were a fair number of people in the ground willing to sit out there and wait with us.

Even had the sun broken through I doubt very much if we could have started that day. Where I felt the crowd were let down was in the public announcements. On occasions such as these I believe it is only fair that the public should be told that play is unlikely even when the final decision to call it off hasn't been taken.

At Old Trafford the people in the stands were told only when the next inspection would take place. The members in the pavilion get to know anyway, and after their attitude in this match I can now understand why so many Lancashire players over the years have told me they prefer to play away from the county's headquarters.

Between the Saturday, which was washed out, and the start of the match on the Monday we lost Boycott, who had gone to have a minor operation for a sinus condition. When no Boycott appeared on the Sunday there was, inevitably, a stream of enquiries from the Press. Had he been dropped? He had sworn me to secrecy until the operation had been carried out, and I tried to divert journalists' enquiries by saying he was injured which, in retrospect, wasn't very wise. 'What's the injury? When was he injured? How was he injured?'

Fortunately our public relations chairman, Sid Fielden, got me off the hook. He had to visit the Press box on another matter and told reporters that Geoff had gone into hospital for the sinus operation, 'but he will play tomorrow'.

When Geoff didn't turn up on the Monday speculation was rife again, although the explanation was entirely innocent. It was clear, when he rang me, that he wasn't fit to play with a streaming and, apparently, still bloody nose.

Geoff had already alerted Ashley Metcalfe to take his place but was due to pick up Kevin Sharp; Kevin had to call out his wife Karen to bring him over the Pennines. The Yorkshire dressing room had suspected that Boycs was due to be called in for some kind of treatment, for we kept getting what sounded like medical messages, asking him to call a Mr Pandy – a name which led to many a joke.

Play was at last possible on the Monday morning which was dry. I won the toss on a greenish pitch still containing some moisture, and naturally sent in Lancashire: there's no point in batting first in a two-day match (we had lost one day due to the rain). Jack Bond had said on the Saturday morning, Lancashire not having won a county match all season, that to win 'we shall have to gamble'. I thought I would give them every chance of a gamble and then see whether they would give us an attainable target, in contrast to some of the declarations of recent years.

Graeme Fowler was out in the second over, padding up to Paul Jarvis – a good delivery and an indication of Jarvis's growing confidence. Paul went to take a career-best 6-61, not bad for a lad just past his nineteenth birthday; Martyn Moxon took two superb slip catches and Lancashire were all out for 151.

I didn't anticipate, however, that Yorkshire would be 124-5 at the close of play. Paul Allott pinned us down, and was unlucky, while Steve Jefferies precipitated a collapse, partly redeemed by Phil Robinson and Neil Hartley. I'd had a talk with Kevin Sharp, pointing out that he had been getting out in a silly way all season: going back to cut and being bowled. I asked him if he was becoming complacent.

'Don't relax because you've got 1,000 runs,' I told him. 'Batting at number three you've got to get 1,000. But a good player would then be thinking of 1,500.' He accepted that and said he would have a good rethink about playing all his shots.

Ted Lester asked the Lancashire chairman, Cedric Rhoades, what was going to happen after Monday evening. Cedric replied, 'You declare overnight and then we'll bat on

and on. We won't declare and you won't get a chance.'
Cedric was joking, of course, but the old give-'em-nowt
philosophy of Roses matches lives on.

So, of course, does the tradition of Roses match weather.
After a perfect day on Monday the rain returned overnight,
and by Tuesday morning we were back to the situation we
had had on Saturday, a saturated outfield, patches on the
square, and masses of low grey cloud moving sullenly
across the sky. The match was called off soon after lunch,
enabling us to get away early. As soon as the decision had
been taken the clouds blew away and the sun poured
through again. I remembered Farokh Engineer's words of
long ago, 'God is a Yorkshireman.' If He is, then it seems
He doesn't want us to win too often this summer.

Sunday, 5 August

Lancashire v Yorkshire
at Old Trafford

Lancashire beat Yorkshire by 5 wickets

This was a disastrous performance on Yorkshire's part. The
pitch, I accept, was surprisingly lively for Old Trafford,
especially when we batted, but that cannot take any credit
for an overwhelming and deserved Lancashire victory.
They had just returned from winning the Benson & Hedges
Cup and they played like winners, confident and
commanding.

Yorkshire produced another abysmal batting performance, and after scoring only 124-9 in the 40 overs there was very little hope of holding Lancashire. In came 'Foxy' Fowler to play a characteristic slam-bang innings and the match was all over, on a beautiful day.

Yorkshire's trouble had really begun when Jefferies' lift and unusual left-arm angle accounted for Metcalfe and Sharp very quickly. Martyn Moxon was bogged down, Philip Robinson tried to grind his way out of trouble, and the fiasco ended with run-outs in the final over. I got myself out for 8 trying to sweep Jack Simmons when we needed to step up the scoring rate, and I stand condemned with the rest.

Graham Stevenson had returned to the side and did manage to dismiss Steve O'Shaughnessy for 3 in the 3rd over which, you might have thought, would have cooled Lancashire a little. It had no effect at all on Graeme Fowler: he drove Sidebottom and Stevenson for fours, hit Oldham back over his head for 6, and Lancashire were 50 up in only 10 overs.

With so small a total to defend we needed 3 or more wickets in the first 15 or so overs to have any kind of chance. At 99-4 Lancashire did put the brake on a little, but we all knew there was never any doubt about the result, even if their final 30 runs were spread over 11 overs.

This was Yorkshire's lowest Sunday score for four years.

Leicestershire v Yorkshire

at Leicester

Leicestershire drew with Yorkshire

Geoff Boycott and Chris Shaw were back in the team at Grace Road for a three-day match that began with me in a fit of fury. What seems to have happened is that someone on the Yorkshire Finance Sub-Committee had proposed an economy measure: the players were to travel together in 1985 in a hired coach. Lancashire have done so this year and apparently saved £7,000 in travelling costs.

The rights and wrongs of travelling by coach do not concern me at the moment although I know that such a move, in a county as large as Yorkshire, where homes and grounds are spread over considerable distances, would not be popular with the team. What infuriated me was that the first news of the proposal came from the Press in the form of a question from David Hopps.

Naturally I blazed up. What kind of a club is it where the Press get to know of committee business before the players? At that moment I resolved to apply to address the next meeting of the General Committee, on 12 September. This is only one of several issues I want to raise. (Yorkshire's captain is a member of the Cricket Sub-Committee but is not consulted on other matters. I believe this to be wrong.)

In the meantime I'd played golf with Ashley Metcalfe, among others, and given him a good talking-to on the need to harness his undoubted talents, on getting his head down, and not playing so many airy-fairy shots. I had been warned by Stevenson that the pitch would be green, but I was surprised to see a surface like that. Winning the toss appeared to be the preliminary for a very heartening victory after the first 3 Leicestershire wickets had gone down for 3 runs.

After that we experienced a typical Peter Willey innings – dour, gutsy, never giving an inch. He was in trouble against Jarvis early on, but stuck it out for more than four hours for 85 runs. And while our bowlers were wearing themselves down trying to get Willey out, along comes Gordon Parsons to swing his bat again and reach a second career-best score, both against Yorkshire, in eleven days.

Willey has spent almost all his entire Test career playing against West Indies fast bowlers, so it was a little amusing to hear him sighing for George Ferris and Andy Roberts, both with Leicestershire. One was injured and the other had returned to Antigua. Said 'Will', 'For the first time in my life I could have had a quick black man on my side and he has to be injured!'

We should have made more of our innings, for after the first morning and early afternoon the pitch eased out considerably, but once again we did not bat well. Leicestershire, through Parsons, Paddy Clift, and Ian Carmichael, the latter having picked up a new nickname of 'Hoagy', all bowled a good length and line but on that pitch they should never have been allowed to dictate terms.

But having lost 3 wickets for 103 the innings became pinned down, brightening up only with a last-wicket partnership of 73 in 21 overs between Carrick and Jarvis, in which Paul made a career-best 31. Gratifying as that was, it was a partnership that almost certainly doomed the match to a draw. As Peter Willey said afterwards, if Leicestershire had bowled one of them out sooner they might then have felt they had the time to get a decent lead and bowl Yorkshire out again.

As it was, the time taken up by that partnership meant that neither side was ever going to be in a position to win the match, and so it proved. Leicestershire started the last day 30 behind with 8 wickets standing, and batted out. The *Leicester Mercury*'s correspondent Martin Johnson described it as 'the worst day's cricket in a decade', and I can understand the criticism, but the fact is that neither side felt strong enough to afford to take the risks to win; after that your first duty as captain is not to lose.

There was a silver lining. I was able to give Kevin Sharp a long bowl with his off spin which, as I have mentioned before, is the subject of some hilarity in the dressing room. On this occasion 'Freddy Laker' found a good length and line and did turn the ball, getting his third first-class wicket. Anyway, so proud was Kevin of this performance that he cut out the following morning's scorecard, signed it and sent it off to Nick Cook, Leicestershire's England spinner.

Willey improved on his first innings score with another fortress of an innings, 167 in 361 minutes. He hit us for 22 fours and left me wondering if, in the present state of Yorkshire's batting, and given that length of time, we could have survived against their bowling.

Yorkshire v Warwickshire

at Headingley

Warwickshire beat Yorkshire by 191 runs

Graham Stevenson bounced the ball on the pitch before the
start. It rose about ankle high. I had a premonition, after the
bouncing we had at Leicester, that we would be fielding all
day and, sure enough, we were.

The sad part was that we got away to a reasonable start.
Arnie and Paul Jarvis ran in well, the ball did seam a little
early on and I had a little luck with a run-out, but we
allowed Geoff Humpage to settle in and then get away from
us and that, with 'Thumpage', is fatal: he got a century – by
no means a classical hundred, for it included several shots
that would not be recommended by Warwickshire's coach,
Alan Oakman. But that's Geoff's game: once he's got his
eye in and assesses the measure of the pitch, he's a very
difficult player to contain. He hits the ball very hard and it's
almost impossible to set a field for him, as captains such as
Mike Brearley have discovered in the past.

We lost the match because our batting broke down twice.
No matter how well Chris Old bowled, and he was helped
by the cloud cover on Monday morning, Yorkshire should
never have been dismissed on that pitch for 153 and 183. We
were defeated by good bowling and indifferent batting.

Old finished with match figures of 11-99 and became the first Yorkshireman to take 10 wickets for and against the county in a championship match. He told Tim Taylor of the *Daily Express* afterwards, 'I didn't know I was making history, and I'm sad it should have been against Yorkshire. I would rather have done it *for* Yorkshire than against them. I'd rather be playing for them now, but that was not to be, and I'm enjoying my cricket with Warwickshire.' 'Chilly' also scored 50 in their innings so all round he had a tremendous match against us.

I had hoped we would be set a run chase on the last afternoon, and when Anton Ferreira left the field with a damaged left hand, I half expected Warwickshire to bat on until the match was extinguished. But Norman Gifford was after a victory and he needed time to bowl us out, so the eventual target was 375 to win in 94 overs. It was a big task but by no means impossible. The sky had cleared, there still wasn't much in the pitch, the outfield was very fast and Warwickshire were short of a key bowler. Even when Geoff Boycott and I were batting together the target was still only 4 runs an over. But to sustain a chase to a target of that size you need a very solid start of around 150-1. That gives you a margin for error in wickets. When I joined Boycott, Yorkshire were 80-4 and although we managed to add 52 in 18 overs there just wasn't sufficient strength to continue the hunt.

Nevertheless, Yorkshire could and should have resisted longer. The last 5 wickets fell for 51. I don't want to keep on saying we played badly, yet I can't deny it: we played bloody badly. Even when I try to make excuses for the batting I become exasperated.

True, Martyn Moxon had a bad bruise on a finger of the left hand but it shouldn't have affected his batting – if it did hinder him in any way, he should have said so and not played at all. True, Boycott and Sharp have got 1,000 runs, but what about the rest of us? Well as Martyn has played this season, he still hasn't got 1,000. After that I have the next highest aggregate, and I haven't played as well as I would have liked. Performances from numbers four and five in the order have been patchy, partly because Jim Love, who might have had a magnificent summer on these pitches, was hit first by illness and then by injury, and partly because we have been experimenting with young players like Robinson and Metcalfe.

Sunday, 12 August

Yorkshire v Warwickshire
at Scarborough

Warwickshire beat Yorkshire by 13 runs

Another magnificent pitch at Scarborough, where the transformation from the stodgy surfaces of recent years to the springy surface this year has been remarkable. I decided to leave out Paul Jarvis. He has done very well for us but he has now got a slight strain at the top of the left leg. We have had so many bowlers suffering from injuries this year that when the lads come down for breakfast I'm frightened of looking, in case I see another limp.

As readers know, our normal Sunday policy is to field first. Ted Lester thought we should bat first on this pitch and I agreed: we had already lost two one-day matches to Warwickshire (by lesser margins than 13 runs!) and they had batted first on both occasions. But this time I had no choice. I lost the toss.

We made a good start. Geoff Boycott and Arnie opened the bowling. Geoff is a very negative bowler – invaluable on a Sunday – and he conceded only 18 runs off his first 5 overs: if both my opening bowlers could do that on a Sunday, we would win many more matches. After 10 overs Warwickshire had scored only 31 runs and I was feeling very happy about the situation.

The next 30 overs proved a disaster for us. Warwickshire, led by Humpage (81) again, scored at 7-plus an over, collecting 220 runs, and Phil Carrick bowled his 7 overs for 33 runs. You don't need a scorecard to imagine what happened to our other bowlers: Graham Stevenson bowled 2 overs for 29, Neil Hartley bowled 1 over for 19.

Yorkshire conceded 40 odd runs in 3 overs and the game had been virtually lost in those 18 deliveries. There is very little margin for mistakes in a 40-over contest. What made it worse was the alleged depth of bowling we fielded in that match: seven of the side were reputed to be bowlers. Even then a target of 252 didn't frighten me. I thought we were capable of reaching that on such a good surface with the batting we had available.

Another poor start put the target out of reach almost straight away. Yorkshire were 78-4 when I arrived. Norman Gifford was bowling, and I knew that if we had any hope at all of retrieving the match, then I had to get after him. Fortunately Neil Hartley played extremely well, fiercely attacking Chris Old, while I had to pick the odd ball from Norman. We managed to make it a contest again, but the run rate required was still 8 an over, and to maintain that sequence of scoring demands absolute concentration, and a lot of luck, scoring off virtually every ball.

It was a very tall order and we seemed to be losing by a big margin when Carrick came in to hit a ferocious 40, including 3 sixes in the last 3 overs. An extra 20 runs – that's all that was needed – from our first three wickets would have clinched it.

Once again the crowd was disappointed by the result. But no one could complain about the entertainment. I was saddened by yet another unnecessary defeat but thankful that there was no repetition of the nasty incidents that had

134

occurred during the Gloucestershire match on the same ground. On another hot day the committee's decision not to open the bars until 4.30 p.m. proved to be the right one. There was no trouble whatsoever; the crowd was good-natured, excited and there wasn't a word or a gesture out of place. It was good to see such a large number of families and children on the ground.

This weekend I had a chance to talk to Geoff Boycott and discuss the various rumours rumbling around at the moment. The main one is that he wants the captaincy. Geoff said he believed that all these stories emanated from outside the club, and that some people were trying very hard to drive a wedge between us. I can believe that. Geoff was quite adamant that he did not want to become Yorkshire's captain again. He had eight years in the job and that was enough for him.

What has been said on the committee I do not know. At the August meeting of the General Committee my captaincy was given a unanimous vote of confidence. Yet I am disturbed by these rumours. Any captain in his first year feels vulnerable, and under scrutiny the whole time.

Saturday, 18 August – Tuesday, 21 August

Yorkshire v Surrey
at the Oval

Surrey beat Yorkshire by an innings and 195 runs

I was still so incensed at our defeat by Warwickshire, and losing by such a large margin on a pitch we should have been able to bat out upon, that I ordered everyone into the nets at Headingley before we picked the team for four days' play against Surrey.

I was particularly concerned about the batting. I know that much of the blame for Yorkshire's defeats this year has been heaped on the bowlers, but my own feeling is that in recent games the batsmen were more to blame.

Kevin Sharp greeted me this morning with the words, 'Boycs has got a hamstring.' Apparently he had complained of a strain after batting in a benefit match yesterday. 'Does that mean he isn't coming, then?' I asked Kevin, meaning that I didn't expect him at the nets.

'Yes', said Kevin. 'He's seeing Paddy Armour [a Wakefield physiotherapist] at one o'clock.'

So we set off for a profitable net exercise, the only alarm coming from Martyn Moxon, who was pulling his left hand away every time he hit the ball. I asked physiotherapist Sarah Butterworth why Martyn's hand was so sensitive. She assured me that it was no more than bad bruising and would ease considerably within twenty-four hours. I told Martyn, as a precaution, that I would take an extra batsman and I rang Mr Armour for a check on Boycott. He reported, 'He's travelling down and I've given him a course of exercises to do so he'll be able to decide in the morning.' My interpretation of that was that Boycott was almost certain to play and that Martyn had a good chance. The travelling reserve was Neil Hartley, who had been having trouble with his back and wasn't fully fit himself. As it happens, however, we were lucky enough to have thirteen in the party.

When I got to the Oval on Saturday morning Boycott had already arrived, changed and walked out. He was told the pitch looked firm, though without a lot of bounce, and went off to do a lap. I didn't see him run but I was told he looked fine. He then returned to the dressing room and surprised me completely by announcing, 'Stanley, it's no. I'm not fit.'

A check on Martyn revealed that he was still feeling pain in his left hand so there we were, about to face Sylvester Clarke and Teddy Thomas without an opening batsman. Given the circumstances, I think the architects of the Surrey pavilion deserve to be congratulated on their sound design. The roof stayed on.

We still required reinforcements. I eventually got hold of Philip Robinson at his home in Keighley and told him I needed him to travel down straight away in time to play on Sunday. Said Philip, 'But I've already agreed to play for Keighley.'

It was a tricky point. Philip was not a contracted player and was quite within his rights. Yorkshire having dropped him, he could tell me to go take a running jump. But he's a sensible lad who wants to make cricket his career and didn't need too much persuading. I then told Boycott and Moxon they could return home on Sunday for treatment, Boycott helping me out by managing to locate Steve Oldham.

By Monday morning, reading the Press, we learned that we were in the middle of another crisis. The panic was such that the *Sun's* cricket correspondent, Steve Whiting, was taken off another match and sent rushing down to the Oval to investigate the latest 'Yorkshire bust-up'.

Brian Close, according to another account, was hurrying down south to sort it all out. In fact, Close was due in London for a business appointment and had arranged to see us at the Oval long before the team had been chosen. He met Ted Lester and myself on the Monday and I told him how pleased I was that he could see at first hand how we were trying to cope with the weaknesses in the side. There was no 'quiz' or 'investigation' or 'inquest', it was a straightforward pre-arranged cricket meeting.

Yorkshire had been bowled out for 183 on the Saturday, and we knew we had a difficult task in trying to contain Surrey to anywhere near that total on what was a good batting pitch and fast outfield. Close wished us luck and made a few points, such as giving the bowlers short spells. It was sticky and humid – what we would call a Durban Day – which may explain why we spilled two early catches and let Alan Butcher and Graham Clinton get away to big hundreds.

The best of our work that day was Kevin Sharp's off-spin. He managed to keep a good line outside the off-stump of the two left-handers, which meant they had to fetch the ball, with the attendant risks, if they wanted to score.

By Tuesday morning we knew we were in danger of a heavy defeat. The pitch was deteriorating, an advantage that would have been ours if we had only batted sensibly and well in the first innings. In the meantime, before play started, we had to choose a side to play Derbyshire at Chesterfield the next day.

Close wrote down a list of the players available and their various states of fitness and form. I rang Joe Lister at Headingley to find out how Geoff Boycott and Martyn Moxon were progressing. He told me, 'There's a net going on outside at present. I'll let you know later.'

I assumed from that, wrongly as it turned out, that both Boycott and Moxon were having a net. As I was waiting to go in to bat, I asked Close to take the call from Headingley. He replied, 'You get on with the game. I'll take care of that.'

We had already discussed the fitness of Hartley, who has consistent trouble with his back after bowling, and Carrick, who has a leg strain that severely restricts his mobility. Close had said, 'O.K. Let them have a rest'. Graham Stevenson was dropped into the second team in another attempt to find some consistent form. Steve Oldham was called back into the first team because we knew he could close up one end, and because we felt he had a point to prove against Derbyshire, the club that released him last year. The real problem was the batting.

When Close did speak to Lister, the news was that there would be no news on Boycott's fitness until after 1.00 p.m. Close said immediately, 'We can't wait. If the team are bowled out early today David will be on his way north not knowing what kind of a team he can field tomorrow. If Geoff doesn't know whether he's fit now then he can either rest the strain for the next three days or play in the second team at Barnsley. It's up to him.'

Naturally the media made much of this, shouting that Boycott had been dropped. In fact, we were merely continuing the policy begun earlier in the season of insisting a player proved himself fit before returning to the first team.

Boycott wasn't dropped nor, as some newspapers claimed, was he given a guarantee that he would automatically return to the first team against Glamorgan on Saturday. That was nonsense. How were we to know he would be fit by then if the hamstring strain was severe enough to keep him out of the Surrey match?

This account of the Surrey match has to be rambling in order to explain what was going on off the field and to put it in some kind of sequence. Back on the Saturday morning, when I had found myself without an opening batsman, the dressing room was, as you can imagine, a hive of conversation. What cheered me immensely was that at least half a dozen of the team volunteered to go in first; the spirit was there.

Young Ashley Metcalfe was the designated number three and the obvious choice to move up to number one, but I was reluctant. He has a great talent but plays far too many shots too soon. In a couple of years, when he tightens up, we shall have a real player but for the moment I would like to bring him along gently.

I turned over in my mind all the options and then decided that the opening partnership would have to be Ashley and Arnie Sidebottom. Arnie plays the new ball well, is a far better batsman, technically, than he might appear and he would give the partnership a little experience.

And we began well enough. Both settled in and I could sense that Surrey, thinking the pitch green and lively, were beginning to wonder if they had made an error. In fact the pitch was neither fast nor bouncy and our problems arose more from Teddy Thomas than the feared West Indian, Sylvester Clarke. What really undermined that middle of the order was the bowling of Pat Pocock, newly recalled by England, and demonstrating what a class spin bowler can do by variation of pace and length when he cannot win any turn.

Geoff Boycott would have been invaluable on that pitch, just to demonstrate to our players how to cope with Pocock. I felt very sad to hear the jibes flying around the Oval that Boycs had suddenly been afflicted with a 'Sylvester Leg'.

When we bowled, as I have mentioned, we put down catches, we let Butcher and Clinton pile on runs and there were moments when I felt I was directing bows and arrows against lightning. By the time we came to bat again the pitch was still flat but there was a little turn, and every now and again a ball from one of the seamers would suddenly balloon. We were utterly smashed, and went north to Chesterfield with heavy hearts.

Yorkshire v Surrey

at the Oval

Surrey beat Yorkshire by 12 runs

Roger Knight asked me if I would help his benefit by saying something over the public address system at the Oval. 'Certainly', I replied. 'If we can bat first.'

I was sorry in a way that Roger, a good friend, was unable to make a century against us in the championship match, as Yorkshire were the only county against whom he had failed to score 100.

Steve Oldham rejoined us for this John Player League fixture but we still had the gap left by the opening batsmen. I said, a few years ago, that I never wanted to go in first for Yorkshire; just a feeling that it wasn't really my place. But this was no time for those kind of sentiments. In fact, I quite enjoyed it and we were away in reasonable fashion, 40 for no wicket.

Then, as we have done so often in recent weeks, we fell apart in the middle. We haven't built on the foundations and our recent Sunday results have been flattering. We have scored runs towards the end of the innings that made the result look closer than it was; i.e. losing by a dozen runs when the real margin was 30 or 40.

As you will have gathered, Roger Knight won the toss,

Surrey batted first and their total of 205-7 was by no means unbeatable. What we didn't expect was some devastating catching by Monte Lynch, four crackers, the best of which was a thirty-yard dash along the long-on boundary, followed by a dive to catch out Graham Stevenson. Without Monte's almost superhuman catching that day we would probably have won this match, which would have alleviated some of the pain on Monday and Tuesday!

I ought to mention Phil Carrick's 43 not out, one of many of Fergie's valiant attempts to boost our scoring rate from late in the innings.

Wednesday, 22 August – Friday, 24 August

Yorkshire v Derbyshire

at Chesterfield

Yorkshire beat Derbyshire by an innings and 30 runs

After all our troubles, or reported troubles, in a long weekend in London, we returned to Queen's Park, the scene of the punch-up during the John Player League match. Roger Pearman, Derbyshire's chief executive, took the trouble to assure us there would be no further trouble, as indeed there wasn't. But, of course, the spectators who watch championship matches are on the whole a different breed from those who attend only one-day matches.

It was a very overcast morning and if I had won the toss I intended to send Derbyshire in to bat, so I wasn't too pleased when I lost. I'd seen Steve Oldham swinging the ball all over the shop in the nets and thought, when I called wrongly, 'Here we go again. We could be rolled over.'

In fact, we made one of our best starts of the entire summer and were always ahead of the over rate, on target even for 400 in the day with Kevin Sharp playing superbly. Philip Robinson and Ashley Metcalfe also played well. Martyn Moxon was the only one who really failed and I felt a lot of sympathy for him. He was under a great deal of pressure all season being tipped, every other day, to play for England. Then he cracked a rib at Northampton, had to drop out of the England side and, apart from a fine 100 under difficulty against Worcestershire, he has hardly made a good score. Another injury to his left hand hadn't helped and he was then left to ponder and worry about whether he would be taken on England's winter tour.

I had no intention of declaring on that first day. The ball continued to swing and 450 is always an attractive target for the side batting first because the opposition then know they need 300 – maximum bonus points in 100 overs, if you like – to avoid a follow-on.

It was clear, too, that the longer the match continued the more help there would be for the spinners. Geoff Miller was making the ball turn quite a lot even on the first day.

We didn't quite achieve our target. Roger Finney, bowling with the new ball at our legs, pinned us down. When it came to Derbyshire's turn to bat, I didn't give the new ball to Paul Jarvis, as expected, but to Steve Oldham, knowing that he would move it a lot and also knowing he was dying to show his old team-mates what they were missing.

It worked, too. Kim Barnett and John Morris both went to drive and edged catches, so that they were two down almost before they had started. Steve and Arnie kept up the pressure and I was then able to use the two spin kids, Paul Booth and Ian Swallow, together in a championship match for the first time. Paul bowled really well from the Lake End. Only Bill Fowler put up any prolonged resistance, and

143

after our crash against Surrey it was a relief to have our next opponents following on.

We were up against the additional pressure that Geoff Boycott was playing up the road at Barnsley for the second team. Some members of both the national and local Press decided that this match was more important than our game in Chesterfield. If the Press say Geoff Boycott is bigger than Yorkshire, well, who has made him bigger? The whole Yorkshire dressing room was disgusted by this attitude. Apparently the team were trivia and the Yorkshire cricket world revolved around one man. What it did do for the team was to stiffen their resolve to play that much harder to prove that it was possible to win, and win handsomely, without Boycs. I say this without intending any reflection on the man himself. He didn't ask the Press to turn up at Barnsley.

On a pitch upon which it became increasingly difficult to bat we were able to dominate the match and win comfortably by a huge margin.

The last day had little stories all of its own. We were in a position to win if the weather would allow it and we pegged away, all the time watching for the rain. John Hampshire is retiring this year, so when his big mate Steve Oldham (they went to Derbyshire together) found an edge, he grinned down the track at 'Hamps' and called out, 'Ge'r'off. That's one for the rocking chair.'

Bob Taylor is also retiring this year and when he and Devon Malcolm, who won a Derbyshire contract after bowling Geoff Boycott in a pre-season match, came together it looked for a while as if they were going to deny us a win.

Then, with 11 overs to go, Bob must have had a mental block, because he suddenly chased young Swallow down the track, missed, leaving me with an easy stumping. I felt rotten about it, dismissing one of the greatest wicket-keepers the world has ever seen and such a gentleman, too, in the way of amateurs.

We tried to compensate for this. I'd alerted the lads, and

as soon as the last wicket fell we hurried across to the pavilion and formed two lines to applaud Taylor off. Only a little tribute from Yorkshire, perhaps, but we wanted to indicate how we felt about him. More than one of us had a lump in the throat.

Saturday, 25 August – Tuesday, 28 August

Yorkshire v Glamorgan
at Bradford

Yorkshire drew with Glamorgan

The last thing I wanted to see at Park Avenue was a green pitch. Glamorgan had fast bowler Winston Davis returning after playing with West Indies. And anyone looking for a fast bowler – and who isn't? – should watch Greg Thomas. The lad is big, strong, genuinely quick and on a slow, placid Bradford pitch he was very lively and a handful. I think he is a tremendous prospect and can only wish he was born in Gomersal.

Park Avenue was a spinners' pitch, and that nearly proved our undoing because Glamorgan won the toss and batted first, which meant we had to bat as the pitch was offering some turn. They really threw their advantage away on the first day when we bowled something like 120 overs and they could score at no more than 3 runs an over.

Perhaps we had too good a start. Alan Lewis Jones was

leg before; I caught Geoff Holmes; John Hopkins gloved one, the ball bouncing just in front of me, leaving me wondering if I'd hit a black cat on the way to the ground.

We were a little weary. We had spent so much time in the field at the Oval and Chesterfield and then, to our dismay, Glamorgan continued batting on the Monday morning, no doubt hoping to build a total that would make them invulnerable.

By the time we did get in to bat it was obvious that they were already getting a great deal of turn from the Football End. The danger was that if our batting collapsed and we had to follow on, Glamorgan had enough bowling and a receptive pitch to help them to a considerable victory.

We struggled. Geoff Boycott played well until given out off bat and pad, but our real star was Philip Robinson. He hit Winston Davis for 23 in 2 overs and then took 20 in 1 over off Ontong; no slogging, clean calculated hitting, all good shots. With Arnie Sidebottom helping we eventually finished only 20 behind on the first innings. Neither Arnie nor I was amused to read his innings described as 'fortunate' in the papers the next day. He had a little luck, and you needed it on that surface, but he played well.

Things went wrong for just about everybody the following morning. Glamorgan restarted with an overnight lead of 40 and lost wickets straight away, so quickly in fact that by lunch there seemed to be every chance that they would be bowled out. I was hoping that as neither county had any chance of winning the championship and therefore nothing to lose, they might have left us 50 overs to get 250-60 but the innings droned on and on.

When the declaration arrived eventually after tea, giving us a nonsensical target, I told Robbo to put on the pads while I had a bowl. When I wandered down to the boundary one spectator told me that the exhibition was a disgrace to Yorkshire cricket. I replied, 'Sir, the only disgrace in Yorkshire cricket this year has been the racial abuse of coloured players by Yorkshire crowds.'

So the match ended with the crowd booing Glamorgan

and slow handclapping. There were a few hard words said and written afterwards, particularly by Derek Hodgson (whoever he is) in the *Daily Telegraph* asserting that Ontong was right not to declare and that it was up to Yorkshire to bowl Glamorgan out twice, not moan about delayed declarations.

The point was also made that Ontong was inhibited from declaring by an arm injury to his other spinner, John Steele. It's true that Steele would have been needed but I do know that when he arrived back at Park Avenue after a precautionary visit to a hospital, he said he was surprised to hear that Glamorgan were still batting. I read that to mean that Glamorgan never had any intention of declaring until they were completely safe.

It's true that our spin kids could have bowled better in helpful circumstances, but they are still learning the trade. Once Glamorgan had decided on a draw, I don't think there's much more we could have done about it, no matter what the *Daily Telegraph* says.

Yorkshire v Glamorgan
at Leeds

Glamorgan beat Yorkshire by 3 wickets

Having left Phil Carrick out of two championship matches, partly to rest his leg (he was far from pleased at missing Bradford), I intended to restore him for his experience and all-round qualities in the Sunday match.

As we walked out to look at the pitch, I noticed little tufts of grass here and there, made a few enquiries and discovered, to my horror, that we were using a strip on the re-laid Test pitch for the first time.

Our experience of re-laid Test pitches at Leeds has taught us to duck! The ball normally flies off a length. Glamorgan had five left-handers in their side, so I decided that Phil Carrick would have to stand down again. This would be a seamer's pitch and over quickly. How wrong can you be?

The ball seamed a little at first, but as soon as the spinners Steele and Ontong appeared, the ball went crazy: Ontong was making it pitch outside the off-stump and clearing the left shoulder. Four or five balls went straight through the top. John Derrick, who is slow medium, hit Neil Hartley on the chest, the ball flying to third man for four byes. I was caught at backward point off a ball that hit the splice. It was by far the worst one-day pitch I've ever played upon.

148

I expected to do much the same to Glamorgan but we had no off-spinner and, to make things worse, Chris Shaw damaged his right hand in his second over and left the match. When a specialist bowler breaks down on a Sunday it's almost impossible to fill the gap, the margins in a 40-over game being so fine. In all the circumstances I was pleased and proud of the team; they tried hard enough but it was rather like climbing uphill into a stiff wind.

Wednesday, 29 August – Friday, 31 August

The Asda Challenge
at Scarborough

Yorkshire beat Derbyshire by 122 runs

Hampshire beat Yorkshire by 7 wickets

Four counties compete annually for the £5,000 prize (with handsome individual awards) and the two semi-finals saw Yorkshire against Derbyshire and Lancashire against Hampshire. Lancashire won the competition in an exciting finish the previous year.

Heavy rain overnight had managed to seep through the covers, leaving a damp patch about two yards wide and a yard long, on a length at the Press Box End. It was obvious therefore that the batsmen of both sides would have difficulties as the ground dried under hot sunshine and a fairly stiff breeze.

149

In these circumstances I wanted to field first. At the toss, I called tails, but as the coin dropped it rolled. There is something of a superstition among cricketers that if the coin rolls it will come down heads and sure enough it did. Yorkshire were put in to bat first.

Early on we didn't experience a great deal of trouble. Ole Mortensen (repeat Ole) and Roger Finney made the ball swing, but as soon as the tall left-hand spinner Dallas Moir appeared the ball began to go crazy, bouncing and leaping. We weathered the storm very well, nevertheless, principally through a very fine late innings from Phil Carrick who played some splendid shots in his 39 not out. I was pleased with what I regarded as an excellent 220-7 in our 50 overs.

My tactics were obvious. As soon as we had used the new ball I put Steve Oldham on at the Press Box End to block their scoring, and attacked with Carrick from Trafalgar Square.

Derbyshire had reached 39 without loss in 9 overs when Kim Barnett fell to a superb catch by Neil Hartley. I then called on Martyn Moxon to field slip to Carrick's bowling and he took three fine catches, two of which were in the Phil Sharpe class. Derbyshire lost their last 9 wickets for 41 runs in 26 overs, 'Fergie' taking 5-13 in 9 overs, 5 of which were maidens. If he hadn't been slogged for a four and two in one over by Bruce Roberts he would have finished with 5-7.

John Hampshire and Bob Taylor, making their last appearances at Scarborough, both got a great reception from the crowd.

I dismissed Bob Taylor with what I may be allowed to say was a good catch, one-handed, a full-length dive to my right; my chief satisfaction in that being that Bob finished his last innings in Yorkshire in some style. I felt that however Yorkshire got him out that day it had to be done in a way that was worthy of his own achievements; anything less would have demeaned the occasion.

On the following day Lancashire put up a rather disappointing performance against Hampshire, losing by

150

43. But the crowd had every reason to expect an excellent final between Hampshire and Yorkshire on the Friday. Alas, once again Yorkshire showed their inconsistency. We batted first and batted badly. Neil Hartley, Jim Love and I had to make up for some erratic play by the earlier batsmen even to reach 219-7. As usual, Phil Carrick made another brave attempt to pull the game round with a not-out 34.

The pitch by now had levelled out into another good batting surface and Hampshire, quite rightly, took full advantage of it. Mark Nicholas and David Turner hit 102 off the first 22 overs and we knew then that unless a miracle happened the Asda Challenge was lost. By the time we got rid of David Turner he had scored 81, Hampshire had reached 171 and with 13 overs left they were able to coast home.

Asda have to be congratulated on promoting an excellent competition. Crowds of around 6,000 were attracted each day, the players were well pleased and word filtered down to the dressing room that such was the hospitality in the Press box that some of our regular critics were as sponsored as newts. Yorkshire certainly hope to be playing in the competition again.

D.B. Close's XI v Sri Lanka

at Scarborough

The match was a draw

I was delighted to be able to play in this match. First, it was good to see Brian Close, Yorkshire's great championship winning captain of the 1960s, leading a side again. Secondly, I was able to play with Desmond Haynes and Roger Harper of West Indies. Third, it was good to be on the same field as the Sri Lankans, the friendliest of teams and excellent cricketers.

Desmond had a poor tour of England by his standards, redeeming it with that steady century at the Oval. He still played like a batsman not quite at his best, although his class and power were all too obvious when he did let the bat go. The Press described him as 'toiling' the following day, and I suppose that 111 in 4 hours 15 minutes was slow for a player they call the 'Hammer'. There wasn't much that was sluggardly about his fourteen boundary shots.

The real surprise to me was Harper, not so much his off-spin, but his arm ball, delivered with such venom that he surprised both me, standing up, and Martyn Moxon, at slip. I have nasty bruises on the arm and chin to prove it: the first one he delivered gave me such a shock that Mike Watkinson, at mid-off, nearly fell over laughing when he saw the expression on my face.

Half seriously I asked Roger if he ever bowled a bouncer, but his reply was 'Certainly, if the pitch is fast enough'. I only hope, if I'm the keeper, he lets me know first.

Harper is, according to the West Indians, the world's best fielder. Was he better than Clive Lloyd in his prime, I asked Desmond? 'No, man.' But he's a pretty devastating man to have anywhere in the field with his reach and speed. The sight of Close and Mushtaq, both rather rotund, crouching at slip, while the 6 ft 8 inch Harper was mooning around the outfield caused a few smiles.

Desmond told me that Harper could cover 100 yards in under 11 seconds. Someone then had the cheek to ask the skipper if he could run 100 yards.

The other memory of the match was Martyn Moxon's three Sri Lankan wickets. He had bowled only gingerly since that rib injury. On this occasion he felt he could let the ball go and he really made it seam. The balls that dismissed Amal Sila and Kuruppu were gems. I pray he can do that for Yorkshire next summer.

Wednesday, 5 September – Friday, 7 September

Yorkshire v Hampshire
at Scarborough

Yorkshire drew with Hampshire

The long dry summer broke at North Marine Road, where high winds and occasional heavy showers made this match more familiar to English cricketers. We'd come down for breakfast never knowing for sure whether we were going to start on time. It came as a considerable shock to Mr Sidebottom, idling over his bacon and eggs, to learn that play would start at 11.00 a.m. on the second day.

The rain had been so heavy that there had been seepage under the covers again and the pitch was wet, but it didn't do as much as we had thought towards helping the bowler. The TCCB frowns on collusion between captains but it is important to have a good idea of what your opponent is thinking, and both Mark Nicholas and I were determined on making this a game of cricket. With this in mind I was delighted to win the toss and send in Hampshire.

They responded with a stand of 113 in 34 overs. Arnie, as ever, might have had a little more luck in his opening spell, but otherwise our bowling lacked length and line. Graham Stevenson had a poor start but improved when given the Trafalgar Square end, from which Steve Oldham also contributed a useful stint. With Nicholas hitting us for another 70 and Robin Smith adding a 62, Hampshire raised 254-6 in 80 overs leaving us just enough time to get into trouble.

Martyn Moxon started handsomely with two boundaries in the first two overs and I was just thinking that he'd found form again when he was caught behind. Boycott was dropped by the wicket-keeper and we were relieved to be 108-1 off 37 overs to close.

That evening our principal sponsors, Servowarm, gave an end-of-season reception. But before this we had a private little ceremony in the Yorkshire dressing room. We presented Richard Lumb, before his retirement to South Africa, with an inscribed watch, a gesture that had him all choked up. We also presented Bill Alley, the retiring umpire, with a bottle of gin. A few laughs, and a lot of sentiment and the feeling another summer had almost gone.

To make a match of it, I had to declare immediately the following morning, presenting Hampshire with a lead of 146. Under the two-day rules Mark Nicholas could have enforced a follow-on but that would have meant that Yorkshire would have no option but to try to bat out the day, which would have led to some pretty dull cricket.

So Hampshire then batted until lunchtime which left us to score 302 to win in 73 overs, a very fair declaration. The pitch was in reasonable shape and the outfield had dried out considerably so that we had to think we could win. Once again we got away to a poor start and never really recovered. Both Moxon and Love had gone for 21 runs, Boycott did his anchorman's job for 39 runs in 27 overs and then Sharp, who looked to be playing well enough to win it for us, got himself out once again by being bowled, cutting. The two Hampshire spinners were now winning a little purchase, Metcalfe was bowled for a duck and although our last five wickets all made a meaningful contribution, we were never in a strong enough position to force the pace for victory.

At the death our last pair, Arnie Sidebottom and Steve Oldham, hung on for 11 overs to force a draw. They played superbly and a good crowd, on a day of mixed weather, enjoyed the cricket. I thanked them for attending and hoped they would watch us next year, thinking to myself that if we were given opportunities like that again we would have to make more use of them.

Saturday, 8 September

Sussex v Yorkshire
at Hove

The match was eventually drawn

It is 334.4 miles from Scarborough to Hove, which is too far to expect any team to travel after a late finish, but the fixture planners do this regularly to Yorkshire. I drove down with Geoff Boycott and was stopped by the police near the M11. I knew I had been speeding and put as brave a face as possible on it, getting out of the car, walking over to the police car. The traffic cop was very polite, 'Do you know what the speed limit is on this stretch of road, Sir?'

I replied, even more politely, being frightened to death, 'I think it's seventy miles an hour.' He looked at me very carefully then nodded his head and said, 'It is for everybody else. On your way, Sir.'

I slumped back into the driving seat with an enormous sense of relief. Boycs then proceeded to tell me of his being stopped once when driving from the Barnsley ground to his old home at Fitzwilliam. A flashing blue light shot past and flagged him down, the copper walked across and smiled, saying 'Ah, hello Geoff, it's you is it?' Boycs then hurriedly explained that he had been practising at Shaw Lane, the officer cutting him short by saying, 'Well, get on with you home. Drive safely. It's a pity you don't bat as fast as you drive.'

I wouldn't want anyone to jump to the conclusion that cricketers are favoured by the police: the number of speeding endorsements and breathalyser tests at any county cricket club will tell you otherwise. But because of the life we lead in the summer, long journeys, tight schedules, a hundred social invitations, we always drive at high risk.

The sense of relief at my motoring escape didn't last for long. The pitch at Hove was so green we wouldn't have known where to start without the stumps. When I lost the toss and told the dressing room we were batting I had many volunteers for the job of twelfth man.

Yet the pitch wasn't so dangerous after all. Boycott and Moxon put on 149 for the first wicket, the sixth time they've passed 100 this summer. Martyn confirmed what we had suspected at Scarborough, he had recovered his form. He scored 84, including 16 fours and had reached his 50 when Boycott was on 17! More important, he passed 1,000 runs for the first time in this, his first full season.

It was a landmark for him that I would have wished for three weeks earlier, because achieving it would have relaxed him. He's spent much of the summer wondering when he would play for England and then whether his injuries would clear up in time for him to pass 1,000 runs. It's a magical figure for a professional cricketer.

Bad light, as we expected, ended play early, but not before Yorkshire suffered another almost inexplicable batting collapse in mid-order. Our bowling, rightly, has taken much criticism but in the last six weeks the batting has been equally to blame. The number three position, vacated by Bill Athey, has never been filled properly and from that weakness the whole of the middle batting seems to have become undermined. It's something we shall have to think about very seriously before the start of next season.

157

Sussex v Yorkshire
at Hove

Match abandoned: Sussex beat Yorkshire on the faster scoring rate

For the second time in two days I lost the toss, so that finally put paid to any thoughts I had of using my luck on a holiday in Las Vegas. It was just as important to win the toss today as yesterday because the over-riding consideration was the weather.

The star was undoubtedly Geoffrey Boycott who, firstly, reeled off 8 overs for 19 runs. Then, when we batted after Sussex had scored 212-5 in their 40 overs, he played some superb shots, including a straight six, back over the head of Colin Wells. He was out charging down the pitch. Otherwise the batting let us down again, although it was a slightly artificial situation in that we knew that it was unlikely that the match would be finished and that we had to risk wickets to chase the Sussex scoring rate.

So Yorkshire, the 1983 John Player champions, finished level with three other clubs second from bottom of the table. A profound disappointment, after a good start, but one that reflected fairly accurately our form over the second half of the season.

I could say to myself that I was ending the summer on no

false notes of optimism. I had learned a lot, including how to be realistic. Servowarm, the sponsors who deserve a lot of credit for standing by the club during an acrimonious winter, had made me Player of the Season, which surprised me. I would have nominated Kevin Sharp. But I was certainly the player who had heard more, seen more and learned more. I enjoyed it. I wouldn't have missed it for the world.

Epilogue

That's it. It's 12 September, the season's over. It seems a light year from that first morning at Taunton back in April. What have I learned? What have I won? What have I lost?

The first lesson, a hard one and patently obvious to anyone who has captained a cricket team, taught me that it is impossible to run with the hare and hunt with the hounds. You cannot make the decisions necessary to run a team successfully without upsetting someone. You cannot stay friends with everyone.

I also discovered that keeping wicket and leading the side, no matter what the critics may say, wasn't as difficult as I expected. Of course there were occasions when mistakes were made, even if I wouldn't admit them at the time. There were matches when it seemed nothing would go right, no matter how the team and I tried to put them right.

The consolation I did have, when things did go wrong, was that I could always understand what was happening, why we were losing. If you know what is wrong you are mostly halfway to putting it right.

Perhaps the best moment in the summer, the quiet moment to be remembered and savoured, was after our innings defeat of Derbyshire at Chesterfield when Steve Oldham came across to me. Esso has a lot of experience, he knows the game and he knows cricketers, so I always listen to him carefully. He put his hand on my shoulder and said, 'You've done well, Stanley. You've handled the bowling and the fielding better than at anytime I've played with you. We all got it right this time.'

It may sound a little naive and even childish, but I felt a bit choked up. Everyone who feels they have done something well likes it to be confirmed. You could say I was 'reight chuffed', as they would in Bradford.

In a sense the captaincy became progressively easier. I can admit now that there were times when I had self doubts but when that happens I had to say 'Forget it'. The club had given me the power I asked for, the selection of the team, and it was up to me to make things work. At first it was very hard to tell an old mate that for one reason or another he wouldn't be in the side.

But after a few times I changed tactics, naming the team after a few consultations so that the players read the list. It was up to anyone who objected to seek me out for a chat.

Playing has been very hard, physically and mentally, because I had no intention of giving an inch on my wicket-keeping. I still believe I am a Test match wicket-keeper and intend to prove it. I was only sorry that this summer's Texaco Trophy matches came along when I wasn't on top form. As Ted Lester said to me, 'This selection's come at not quite the right time for you.'

I collected my usual quota of strains, bumps and bruises, adding for good measure this year a strange rash (during the Essex game at Leeds) and a crack on the skull (after being hit on the helmet at Lord's). Worst of all was the back strain that I picked up in August. That affected my wicket-keeping, handicapping my bending, stretching and mobility generally. Before I could take the field, I had to take tablets, have my back sprayed with an anaesthetic and, finally, have the famous Heineken bar towel strapped across my rear.

As to my team-mates, I can't say I've learned a great deal more than I already knew. I realize now that there are different cliques inside the team when it comes to field settings: there are some who want to move fielders to the spot where the ball has just gone, hoping it will go there

161

again; there are some who like 'insurance men', fielders placed in positions for the bad ball. But you can't follow either school. You've got to place your men where the ball should go if everyone does their job properly.

Without doubt Yorkshire suffered one major loss this summer – Graham Stevenson. He is such a good player that I would expect from him about 50 first-class wickets and 500 runs not, I must add, in a consistent compilation of two or three wickets here and 25 runs there but in sudden, dramatic, match-winning bursts. Stevo has that capability. The tragedy of Graham Stevenson is that the only man in the Yorkshire dressing room who doesn't think he is an England player is Stevo himself.

Because of injury and lack of form Stevo was virtually a non-performer for most of the summer. When Arnie Sidebottom had that mid-season spell of shin soreness we were left without an experienced strike bowler and, bravely as Steve Oldham has battled for us this summer, he is no longer a three-day championship bowler. Whatever wickets we have gained through Esso have been bonuses.

The biggest advance in any Yorkshire player came from Kevin Sharp, who really matured as a batsman, passing 1,000 runs for the first time (and batting at number three, which isn't really his spot), who has fielded brilliantly anywhere, and who is starting to look like a promising off-spinner.

Martyn Moxon became a Test player (even if that injury stopped him from actually playing in a Test), but we expected that of Martyn, even in his first season. What was an extra delight was to see him develop almost overnight into a Test-class first slip and a more than useful seam change bowler·

The shock was Philip Robinson, who may not look like a professional cricketer (although full-time training will soon change his shape) but who appeared, at twenty, to play as though he had been performing in first-class cricket since he was fourteen. For a batsman, with no experience outside the Bradford League and Yorkshire II, to enter county cricket and average 40 was phenomenal.

The amazing thing about the bowlers is that so many of them were just names to me when the season started. I had seen Stuart Fletcher in one match, Chris Shaw at the nets and, although Paul Booth and Ian Swallow must have been in view at some time, I had to shut my eyes on the field occasionally and think to myself 'Yorkshire are now fielding an attack that was totally unknown only a few weeks ago.'

That, really, is the reason we didn't do better. The batting had its ups and downs – Jim Love might have had a fantastic season on the 1984 pitches had he stayed clear of illness and injury – but there were always enough batsmen, even if they didn't always perform properly.

There were times this summer when Yorkshire – looking right back to 1863 – can never have been so desperate for bowling strength. That is the major reason why we lost the John Player League championship: to succeed in the Sunday 40-over game you must have a regular team, especially regular bowlers, who know exactly what they have to do even before they take the field.

Our Sunday team was almost always a case of make and mend, a patch here and a patch there. I'm not excusing some poor Sunday performances – and there were some – but I would like to give the lads some credit for the times we did win, often against the odds, like Stevo's mighty assault on Somerset at Middlesbrough, or Neil Hartley's last ball winner against Leicestershire at Bradford.

Yorkshire won five championship matches and should have secured two more. Three championship matches only were lost although, I do concede, when we lost we went with a bang; by an innings to Essex and Surrey, and by a lot to Warwickshire.

We were 4 runs short of appearing in the Benson & Hedges Cup Final. I would rather make no further comment on our progress in the Nat West competition.

Let the dust settle. March, and training again in cold winds and occasional sleet, will soon be here. After that, well, there's not much in life to match a summer's day at the cricket.

Postscripts

On 12 September, the General Committee of the Yorkshire County Cricket Club met at Headingley. The chief item on the agenda was the question of completing contracts for 1985 onwards and the committee had before them the recommendations of the Cricket Sub-Committee.

After a meeting of three and three quarter hours, the committee chairman, Mr Reg Kirk, announced that the present first team players, including David Bairstow, would be awarded new two-year contracts. Geoffrey Boycott and Colin Johnson, the second team captain, were given renewable one-year contracts.

The committee's decision, said Mr Kirk, had been arrived at by a vote of sixteen to one, with four abstentions and four members absent. The Cricket Sub-Committee had awarded all these recommendations 'by a majority'.

As Brian Close was known to be opposed to a new contract for Boycott, unless Boycott gave up his seat on the committee, there was considerable interest in how Close was out-voted in the Cricket Sub-Committee of which he was chairman. It was reported that Mr Kirk, exercising his right as club chairman, had attended the sub-committee meeting and voted.

No decision was taken on reappointing David Bairstow as county captain. 'There had not been time to discuss the matter', said Mr Kirk.

Derek Hodgson
13 September 1984

It was 10.30 p.m. and I was watching *News at Ten* when suddenly Alastair Burnett dropped two bombshells on me. The first was that Geoffrey Boycott had been given a one-year playing contract. Then came the really shattering one: the decision on making me captain again for 1985 had been deferred to a later date.

For the next twenty-four hours all the newspapers seemed able to print was 'BOYCOTT CAPTAIN?' When I went out for a paper or took the dogs for a walk everyone who saw me asked if I had a job next year. I was appalled to be in such a position – I had thought that I had done a reasonably good job for the club in 1984.

The next day I went to Headingley to deliver some papers. I saw the chairman of the club, Mr Reg Kirk, there and told him how I had felt, hearing such important decisions on the television, and he agreed with me that it was a completely unsatisfactory way to find out such news. There is no way that I think I have a divine right to captain Yorkshire Cricket Club, but I did feel when I heard the non-decision that I deserved another chance, and I would like to have been notified in person at that committee meeting of how things stood. The deferral of that decision has caused untold harassment and upset in the Yorkshire cricket set-up.

The club has never said that I would not be captain, but they have not said I would be, either. I feel far too much has been left to speculation. We can only wait and see what will happen over the next few months and whether or not people will go on stirring up the glowing embers of last winter's fire of discontent.

David Bairstow
14 September 1984